The Ghost Hunters Guide

West Virginia Pen

Sherri Brake

Copyright © 2014 Sherri Brake and Raven Rock

All rights reserved.

ISBN: 1492213578

ISBN: 13: 978-1492213574

Printed in the United States of America

Library of Congress CIP data applied for.

Notice: The information in this book is true and complete to the best of our knowledge. It is offered without guarantee on the part of the author or Raven Rock. The author and Raven Rock disclaim all liability in connection with the use of this book.

All rights reserved. No part of this book may be reproduced, stored in a retrieval system or transmitted in any form by any means- electronic, mechanical, photocopying, recording or otherwise, without prior written permission from the publisher or author except in the case of brief quotations embodied in critical articles and reviews.

Cover Design by Raven Rock

DEDICATION

For the seekers of spirit, both light and dark
and what lies beyond.
Enjoy this guide as you walk the darkened hallways.
Be safe and keep an open mind.

Sherri Brake

Books by the Author

Haunted Stark County Ohio (2009)
The Haunted History of the Ohio State Reformatory (2010)
The Haunted History of the West Virginia Penitentiary (2011)
Fireside Folklore of West Virginia Vol. I (2012)
Fireside Folklore of West Virginia Vol. II (2014)
The Haunted History of the Trans Allegheny Lunatic Asylum (2014)
Fireside Folklore of West Virginia Vol. III (2017)

Visit the author's website to view tours, events, ghost hunts and to order books
Haunted Heartland Tours
www.HauntedHistory.net

CONTENTS

Acknowledgments

1	A Brief History	1
2	Death & Torture	11
3	The Executions	21
4	Staff & Volunteer Ghost Sightings	53
5	Paranormal Encounters	61
6	Shadow People Sightings	105
7	Psychic Impressions	114
8	The Gear	128
9	Paranormal Hotspots	138
10	Electronic Voice Phenomena	165
11	Investigation Forms	168

Conclusion

Maps of the Pen

About the Author

ACKNOWLEDGMENTS

♥

For those overnight investigations that you attended and helped with, I thank my husband, Perry. You never complained. You were often a "cell mate" on hunts but always a soul mate in life.

To my kids, Sage and Mason Recco: you continue to inspire me and make me very proud. I am lucky to be your "crazy" mama.

To my parents, Larry and Suzi (Green) Brake; for instilling a hard work ethic that is apparent in all three of their daughters.

Thank you to the Moundsville Economic Council, and the staff and volunteers at the West Virginia Penitentiary. Kudos for all that you do to preserve the history and bring in the tourists.

To the past Wardens, Correctional Officers, staff, teachers, medical personnel and clergy; thank you.

When the past no longer illuminates the future,
the spirit walks in darkness.
Alexis de Tocqueville

CHAPTER 1
A BRIEF HISTORY

Sure, it would be a lot of fun to just jump right in and start your investigation, but any investigator worth their weight in ectoplasm knows that history is the basis and the very foundation and core for any investigation into the paranormal. How can you claim a place to be haunted from prior residents if you don't know who the prior residents were?

As we start this guide to the West Virginia Penitentiary, you must realize that since the prison closed in 1995, thousands have come before you to investigate and explore the very hallways you are about to experience. Many have come away shaking their heads in disbelief at some oddity that befell them on their quest. For others, it was simply a quiet night and although nothing paranormal seemed to happen, they had a very good time and appreciated the building and its history. A few basically could not even make it past the front lobby. They claimed they "felt" darkness, were a bit uncomfortable or were extremely nervous about going past the impressive, hydraulic prison doors. I imagine the sound of a massive door slamming shut behind you (in a prison) would cause many a soul to want to "sit it out." Can you blame them?

The history of the West Virginia Penitentiary is a lengthy and interesting one. I encourage you to check out my previous book, *"The Haunted History of the West Virginia Penitentiary"* if you would like a more in depth look at the most famous prison in the state. This guide book features some of the ghost hunter's sightings and encounters with Shadow People that were showcased in the Haunted History book so please don't think we will leave the good stuff out!

Let's go back to the year 1866. The prison was being built and would open soon to the not so willing occupants. The state of West Virginia was still a "new" state carved out of the great state of Virginia in 1863 and for political reasons we will not go into here, was just in its infancy of development after the end of the American Civil War in 1865.

The West Virginia Pen still under construction in 1876

In 1885 the capital, which had been shuttled back and forth between Wheeling and Charleston, became fixed at Charleston. The capital moved so often in its early years that it was nicknamed the "floating capital." In 1870, the State

Legislature designated Charleston as the capital city. In 1875, the Legislature reversed their decision and voted to return the capital to Wheeling. This was appealed by the citizens of Charleston and finally settled by the West Virginia Supreme Court of Appeals in favor of Wheeling. In 1877 the Legislature ordered an election to be held for the citizens of West Virginia to select a permanent location for the capital, choosing between Charleston, Martinsburg and Clarksburg. By proclamation of the governor, the official move took place eight years later, and in 1885 the capital moved from Wheeling to Charleston, where it has remained. This factored greatly into the placement of the states' very own Penitentiary. Over the years it has been called the State Pen, The Moundsville Pen and a few other unmentionable names I am sure were uttered under the breath of many an inmate.

Needless to say, the prison was built mostly with inmate labor. Blood, sweat and quite a few tears were shed as the early years of the Pen saw more than its fair share of torture, sickness, and death. Hundreds of men died from communicable diseases, punishments from some evil minded guards, poor diet, suicides and murders. This is a sure recipe for paranormal activity. Think of the sadness, feelings of hate and envy and revenge that surely must have permeated many a cell. These emotions can hang on the atmosphere like fog that cannot be seen, only felt. This is called residual energy and the prison has plenty of it. (More on that in another chapter.)

The Architecture

The prison's Gothic type architecture reflects the predominant prison architectural style in England and America at the time of its building. What better style than Gothic for a prison? How imposing it stands today, but can you imagine arriving by wagon back in the old days and seeing those turrets and battlements standing stark against the sky? The massive stone walls and guns pointed at you at every turn and junction?

The design of the Pen was basically modeled after the Joliet Prison in Illinois. It was built from stone in the classic Gothic architectural style, complete with turrets and battlements, just like a castle. Only the dimensions of West Virginia's facility would differ from the prison in Illinois. The Pen would be approximately one-half the size of Joliet Prison. The stone was quarried from Cameron and Rosbey's Rock area in Marshall County and from the town of Hundred in Wetzel County. The solid stone walls were cut and built by the labor of convicts and citizens. The Warden and Board of Directors reports of that time frame indicate that a wooden structure was used at first to house the prisoners, with a wooden stockade enclosing the yard. Many inmates escaped as it was an inadequate enclosure.

From the MEDC collection

Due to the many murders, riots and suicides, the prison nudged itself into an unsavory reputation among correctional facilities. During many of the operational years, it maintained a constant presence on the Department of Justice's Top Ten Most Violent Correctional Facilities. Due to poor record keeping, no one knows for sure how many people lost their lives inside its walls, but a documented 998 men died on the premises and 94 men were executed by the state. Nicknames like "Bloody Alley" and "Hell on Earth" didn't help the Pen's image either, I imagine. Some inmates had unspeakable nicknames for the building...we will just leave it at that.

The Pen was originally built to comfortably house up to 840 male and 32 female inmates. With the Great Depression in the 1930s, the building's census would swell and would hold more than 2,700 prisoners at this time. In overcrowded conditions many cells would house not only two inmates on bunks but a 3rd who would lie on the floor on a mattress.

I am sure as you approached the front of the building on your visit, (or *when* you go) you will notice the massive size of the buildings footprint. The main prison building is five city blocks long by two city blocks deep and sits on about 10 acres of land. The prison yard's basic shape would be a parallelogram 682 ½ feet in length, by 352 ½ feet in width. The yard is enclosed by a solid sandstone wall which is five feet in thickness at the bottom, and about 2 ½ feet at the top. The walls extend into the ground with foundations five feet below the surface. The walls are an intimidating 25 inches thick. At each of the corners of this wall would be large turrets, for the use of the guards, with inside staircases. The center tower section is 682 feet long and it lies at the western side of the building along Jefferson Avenue and is considered the front. This is where the main entrance is located and is where the Wheel structure is located. The walls of the front of the Pen are 24 feet high and 6 feet wide at the base, tapering to 18 inches towards the top of the structure.

The administration area of the West Virginia Pen
Photo by Author 2012

As you stand in front of the Pen and look to the far left, you will see a tall center section of the prison. This is the old administration area which housed the warden and various offices back before the Warden's private house was built in 1951.(This is still standing). The warden lived on site but eventually it wasn't considered safe, or smart for the warden and his family to do so, especially after many uprisings and violence. After all, he was probably the most hated person due to the nature of the occupants housed there. The warden and his family lived in the two upper floors of the Administration Building in a spacious apartment, with large rooms on the fourth floor. The fine woodwork is still evident on doors and baseboards, and the winding stairway although the area is now in great disrepair with falling plaster and crumbling walls.

The Men

The thousands of inmates at the West Virginia Pen had one thing in common. Through the early years and until the closing of the institution in 1995 they were all held *against* their will. Confined in cells behind the stone walls reaching some 20 feet high and away from their loved ones, they dealt with their sentences in many different ways. Some found religion, some cursed God while others turned to the worshipping of Satan. Inmates wrote letters home, scratched poetry and the words to popular songs or bible passages onto the metal walls of their 5x7 prison. Desperate men tried to climb walls with ropes made of sheets, climbed through holes of prison ductwork, dug tunnels or shot their way out. They were prisoners plan and simple. Many deserved this fate, a few were innocent of their crimes and others were rehabilitated and perhaps paroled or released. Some unlucky souls were put to death as a result of their crimes, convictions and sentences. 85 men swung from the rope and 9 were electrocuted in the oak chair known as "Old Sparky."

These men surely had their good days and their bad days just like normal people on the outside. Feelings of shame, hate, hurt, regret, fear, pain and loneliness topped the list and some acted out on these with violent rages against themselves and others. There are 998 documented murders and suicides at this institution and one can only guess at the *true* numbers. I am sure that some accidental deaths by abuse "went away" due to having falling between the cracks of paperwork, neglect or the simple instance of turning your head the other way. Of course these tortuous deaths would have been in the early years of the prison before reform and rehab were instituted practices.

Prisoners in the yard
From the Prison publication "Work & Hope"

The violent feelings these men experiences can be left upon the very atmosphere like a fog of sorts. This residual energy or imprinted energy can be felt by many. I have seen it time and time again on the face of a new visitor as they walk through the lobby doors on their first visit. If you think prison life would be easy at this institution, walk into North Hall at night and sit down on a metal bunk in a cell. Turn off your flashlight and just be still. I can guarantee you will be looking around uneasily after a few minutes alone. Welcome to the Pen.

The Women

This is an often neglected and overlooked fact of the Pen's history; women inmates. Not only were these wayward women incarcerated here but they worked at various jobs during their time. Approximately 80 women prisoners were housed up until 1947, when a new facility was opened at Pence Springs, West Virginia. The Female Department was located in the 1920s at the northeast corner of the North Recreation Yard and was a two-story building with separate dining room and kitchen. Approximately 50 women were employed in part of the shirt shop making collars and cuffs for the shirts made by the men prisoners. The other women were employed in domestic work within the others departments. In other words, women couldn't just sit back and be a prisoner, there was cooking and cleaning that had to be done. Go figure!

Women inmates on a prison picnic
Photo from the MEDC collection

The West Virginia State Board of Control investigated the State Penitentiary at Moundsville in 1944 and their investigation revealed that the States present facilities for women inmates were inadequate and unsatisfactory. At that time, women were being housed in cell blocks identical to those provided for male prisoners. Joseph Z. Terrell, President of the West Virginia State Board of Control, was the Warden at the West Virginia Pen. During that time, he had made several efforts to have the women moved from their cramped and inadequate quarters in one wing of the penitentiary to a facility for women. Upon his recommendation, the 1945 West Virginia Legislature appropriated $203,000 for the establishment of a State Women's Prison.

Subsequently, the State Board of Control obtained an option to purchase a hotel property in Pence Springs, WV for the sum of $45,000. Warden Terrell brought the matter before the interim committee of the legislature, and on May 20, 1946, they recommended that the board exercise the option. This was done and Warden Terrell said that as soon as the building could be remodeled, the 70 to 90 women who have been housed at Moundsville would be transferred to the Pence Springs Hotel. I am sure this was a welcome change for the ladies of the Big House!

Probably the most famous woman prisoner at the Pen was Kathleen Maddox. Kathleen was the mother of serial killer and cult leader, Charles Mansion. In 1939 Kathleen and her brother were convicted of robbing a gas station in Charleston, West Virginia. They had used a glass Coke bottle to knock the attendant unconscious. She was caught and sentenced to five years at Moundsville. Rumor has it that her work assignment was near death row. West Virginia was a hanging state at that time, and part of Kathleen's job was to clean the Death House and that included the area under the hanging scaffold. We can only imagine...

CHAPTER 2
DEATH AND TORTURE

Devices for torture were used to inflict unbearable agony on a victim in the early days and one would think that devices that had been used in medieval days would not have a place in the 19th century Penitentiary in Moundsville, West Virginia. You are dead wrong if you think torture never happened here behind the stone walls.

As far back as 1869, we have documentation questioning torture and discipline practices that were occurring at the prison. The *Wheeling Intelligencer* dated September 13, 1869, mentioned accusations aimed at Warden G.S. McFadden. *In the Wheeling Intelligencer on* September 22nd, 1869, the late Clerk of the Superintendent, Mr. Peter Yarnall, blew the whistle on questionable conditions and barbaric practices at the prison which he was witness to on multiple occasions. During this time frame a United States Inspector visited the prison and demanded that he be allowed to inspect the concerns that private citizens and public officials expressed. Colonel Wilkerson says that Superintendent Peck ordered him to go into the dark cells and to conceal all of the instruments of torture which were in sight. "I went down there," the Captain said, "took all of the whips and other movable instruments of torture and hid them before the officers got there. The 'shoo-fly' was an immovable structure and I could not knock it into pieces as commanded, but everything else was put out of sight. When the officers got around to the cell, which was the last thing shown him by Superintendent Peck, he found nothing but the 'shoo-fly.' The superintendent told him that its use had been discontinued and that all cruel mistreatment of prisoners had been abolished.

Devices and methods used at the prison ranged from the Kicking Jenny, The Shoo Fly and the Weighing Machine. The Kicking Jenny instrument was commonly used to restrict prisoner movement while being whipped. The Kicking Jenny device was described in the November 1886 *Cincinnati Enquirer* newspaper article by past Assistant Superintendent, Captain W. E. Wilkerson as this; "It is made somewhat in the shape of a quarter-circle, with the highest end about three or four feet above the platform upon which it is set. The prisoner is stripped naked and bend over upon the machine. His feet are fastened to the floor with ropes, while his hands, which are stretched over the upper end, are tied with roped attached to small blocks, by which a tension so strong that the frame of the prisoner can almost be torn in two, can be made with a slight pull. After the prisoner is placed in position, the Superintendent, or whoever does the whipping, takes a heavy whip, made of sole leather, two pieces of which, about three feet long, are sewed together and the ends scraped slightly rounding, the lash being three inches broad at the handle, tapering to a point. With the whip the prisoner is beaten until he is almost dead, or the strength of the man who is doing the whipping gives out. I have seen men whipped until they were covered with great purple and red welts from their hips to their shoulders. The lash would make a long welt across the body, and perhaps the next blow would fall across the others, when the blood would let out of the wounds and the victim's back would be one mass of blood, torn and lacerated skin and flesh."

The Kicking Jenny Device

The Shoo Fly was a stationary device that has been described in various newspaper accounts in prison history. I am sure it was horrific to experience as I have a fear of water (specifically drowning) and cannot imagine the fear experienced with this "treatment." The victim would be placed with his feet in the stocks, his arms pinioned and his head fastened so that he could not move it, not even an inch. The punisher would take the large water hose and turn the water fully upon the prisoner's face. This was kept up until the victim was partly strangled to death and partly drowned. Imagine a man receiving a stream of water from an inch nozzle full in the face without the power of changing his position allowed. Torture indeed!

The weighing machine was described in the April 11thth,1886 edition of the Wheeling Register as this; "It is merely a solid oak plank set in a grooved frame, so that it could readily be moved up or down to any height. When it was high enough two iron pins were pushed into the holes in the grooved pieces, and the plank was held fast. A hook was fastened in the center of the plank, to which was fastened a chain connection with a pair of handcuffs. When a prisoner was brought up to be punished in this machine, he would first be handcuffed to the chain. The cross piece was then elevated until the prisoner's toes barely touched the floor of the cell. Thirty seconds of agony is as much as any man in any of the State prisons has been able to bear. Before that time the blood seems to burst from the finger ends, and the nails seem ready to fly from their places. The convict, be he ever so stubborn, shrieks and cries from pain. He is then let down and sent to a cell, often to remain there for weeks and months with swollen wrists and ulcerated wounds."

It is difficult task to secure all of the names of those men who were killed or abused by these devices. Several documentations of this treatment exist with names of the unlucky souls who succumbed to their death by those cruel devices. The names that have been found so far are: John G. Roberts, Louis Heckmer, Joe Paul, W.S. Douglas and John Forsett.

As a paranormal investigator, the more information you can glean from history, the better your investigation can be. With the gathering of names and dates of violent deaths, it gives you more details to tailor your questions in regards to the application of Electronic Voice Phenomena. (For you newbies, this is the gathering of ghost/spirit voice by the use of audio recordings. (See the chapter on *The Gear*)

Improvements?

By the 1920's, changes in prisoner treatment, diet, rehabilitation and sanitary conditions were starting to improve or be implemented. One edition of the *Prisoner's Magazine* called "Work & Hope" was sold at the Pen to visitors for 25 cents, spoke of conditions of past torture such as this; "Underground dungeons in which men were alternately frozen and suffocated were also employed.

Bucking and gagging was another dreadful form of punishment which has likewise been abolished by all humane prison officials. This torture was inflicted usually in the following manner: The prisoner was handcuffed; his hands slipped over in front of his knees, his mouth forced to open and filled with a large piece of cork or wood and left in this condition until life was almost extinct."

The article continued with "But more wonderful that all has been the improvement in prison management and reformative method brought about within the last twenty-five years. No doubt it is hard for citizens of West Virginia to realize what within that time men have been beaten to death, or otherwise slaughtered, while undergoing brutal punishment in their state prison, yet such are the facts."

Inmates lined up for flogging
From Earl Ellicott Dudding's 1932 book "The Trail of the Dead Years"

The article continues, "Since prisons first were built, flogging has been recognized form of punishment for refractory prisoners. There were several methods by which this torture was inflicted. In some prisons the unruly prisoner was forced to stand in front of a post, to which his hands, extended above his head, were tied. Then with a cat-o'-nine tails, a whip of at least nine cowhide lashes, often with wire interwoven so as to cut the flesh with every stroke, a husky prison guard, lashed the prisoner across the bare back. These whips cut deep – each of its burning tongues digging through the skin of the victim. Blood spurted from the cuts as the prisoner howled in pain. Often the flogging went on until the prisoner fainted. Many men have died under the tongue, and there are many men in and out of prison who carry deep scars on their backs caused by the wounds of the cat-o'-nine tails."

The article continued on describing more torture, "Another instrument of torture which was once used in this prison was a big strap about two inches wide made of pieces of harness leather sewed together. When soaked in water overnight, dipped in sand and vigorously applied to the bare flesh this caused most excruciating pain. In this, as well as most all other prisons in the country these forms of punishment have been discarded."

And finally; "It is recorded here that women were paddled in this manner, also. The only difference being that the women were dressed in a very thin gown before the paddling was administered, but this gown was generally torn to shreds before the punishment was over." The Work & Hope magazine really gave visitors the low down on past tortures with some pretty gruesome details. Don't you agree?

Death by Disease

In the early days of the prison, diseases ran rampant especially before the invention of simple antibiotics. Sanitary conditions were in gross neglect with spoiled food sometimes being served to the inmates and inadequate portions of fruits and vegetables. Rats ran everywhere and bedbugs, scabies and lice were common. Morale was low and communicable diseases were raging. Tuberculosis, the deadly Influenza outbreak of 1917-18 and smallpox claimed hundreds of inmates. The hospital census would escalate at these times and many suffered horrible deaths as you can imagine.

*Corner of the old hospital building. (demolished)
From the MEDC collection*

Death at the Hands of Other Inmates?

Murders were numerous at this institution. Take a look at prison records and you get an inkling of the variety of various "accidents" that resulted in death. These are just a few from my 2011 book, "The Haunted History of the West Virginia Penitentiary."

In 1929, inmate Arthur Perry fell to his death.

Ben Thorp died by stab wounds in 1929.

Dallia Cutchshaw was "accidentally" drove over with a truck and died on September 3rd of 1943.

Ross E. Mays died on November 20,1948. His record just says that he "drank hydraulic brake fluid."

Jesse James McNeeley drowned in 1953.

David Lee Poole stabbed to death in 1963.

Toney Santas Jr. died of "accidental poisoning" in 1968.

Jonathan Jenkins died of "accidental poisoning" in 1970.

Floyd Snow died from head injuries in 1977.

Michael McMillion died in 1986 by an inmate's blade.

John Perry suffered death by a crushed skull in August of 1989.

The Taking of One's Life

The word suicide comes from the Latin, suicidium, meaning "to kill oneself." Besides the occasional murder, many inmate suicides occurred at this prison as well. These unfortunate souls, for one reason or another, decided to end their existence in this dimension.

A common religious belief is that suicide is a mortal sin and that the person who dies through self-inflicted violence will go to hell. A violent and tragic death is often believed to lead a troubled soul to become trapped or bound to the physical world and this dimension. One example of this took place in the Aokigahara forest, which is located near Mount Fuji, Japan. The forest is said to be haunted by the ghosts of people who have killed themselves and it is estimated that over 500 people have taken their lives in those woods. In this case, the violent and tragic cause for the existence of ghosts is thought to be due to suicide. According to Japanese myth and demonology, Aokigahara forest is also inhabited by demons.

Suicide is found in various ghost stories, folklore and across many cultural superstitions, and has been strongly associated as one of the more significant causes for restless spirits. In my book, *The Haunted History of the West Virginia Penitentiary*, I shared a few of the documented suicides found in various files. Several of these are as follows;

Inmate # 27687 Benjamin Legg, died in 1942 from self-inflicted skull injuries.

Earl Heavner from Grant County ended his life by committing suicide by drinking antifreeze in 1943.

Thomas Arthur Madison died from drinking ethylene glycol which is commonly found in automotive antifreeze in 1959.

Oley Holsclaw hung himself on May 6th of 1964.

Jerry Moss, Inmate # 48782 swung from his own homemade rope in 1982.

Charles Phillips hung himself in 1988.

Why would an inmate kill himself? The reasons are numerous. Mental illness can and often does lead to social alienation. Combine that to the fact that you are incarcerated and you have increased your chances of becoming a suicide statistic. Diagnosis such as schizophrenia or bipolar depression can confuse rational perceptions and emotions. In such cases, suicidal thoughts can occur or be put into action. A sense of hopelessness can certainly escalate in one's mind and led a prisoner to death by his own means.

By today's standards, suicide is a very complicated issue within the Church. The sanctity of life is recognized in the very act of creation and the taking of one's life is, in many religions a sin. In both the Roman Catholic and Orthodox Churches, suicide is a mortal sin and burial was denied to anyone who took their own life. In some cultures suicide is honorable and even desirable under the right circumstances. Japanese Samurai felt as though ritual suicide was a way to make atonement for dishonoring one's self or one's family.

Paranormal investigators acknowledge that souls can be trapped or stuck between dimensions. Depending upon the religious beliefs of the inmate, this may be a reason while they are still in this dimension or wandering between the veils. Various psychics and mediums have helped several souls cross over. I have been present for some of these events and it is amazing how "light" the air feels after this is completed.

CHAPTER 3
THE EXECUTIONS

The rope and the chair. Either word struck fear into a prisoner's heart. Eight-five hangings and nine electrocutions are imbedded into the fabric of the Pen's history. These men were convicted for their violent crimes and suffered the greatest penalty which was death by hanging or electrocution. The Pen held executions on site from 1899 until 1965 when the death penalty was abolished. The first execution was in 1899 and last execution at the Pen was in 1959. Hangings were the first mode of execution at the prison although many believed them to be inhumane. The majority of inmates received a quick fall to death but there were a few unlucky ones who were decapitated or due to bad judgment in weight or length of rope, suffered for a few minutes before death overtook them.

The first hanging at the Pen occurred on October 10th of 1899 and was that of Shep Caldwell. A select number of citizens were allowed to attend the execution at the discretion of the officers in charge. The general public watched the horrific affair from wooden bleachers on 8th Street. Caldwell was found guilty of murdering his mistress, Rose Henshaw, in Keystone, McDowell County, the previous June. He had committed murder after discovering her with another man.

Just after 1:00 a.m. and in front of about fifty spectators, Caldwell became the first man to die at the hands of the state. Prisoner # 3745 from McDowell County was only 25 years old when he was executed. He was African American and a migrant laborer from the south. He was sentenced on August 4th, 1899, waiting only 2 months and 6 days before the noose was placed around his neck. Crime never pays.

1958 "Old Sparky"
Photo from the MEDC Collection

The Wagon Gate and the Death House

The first hangings were believed to have taken place at the first building constructed on the site, a stone building known as North Wagon Gate. Trap doors were installed on the second floor of the building that would drop the convicted to their death. In the 1920s, the cells for the condemned as well as the execution room were reportedly moved to the Main Hospital Building. When the electric chair was put into use, a new building called the Death House was constructed, which contained four cells (death row) and an execution room on the first floor. A Chaplain's office, library, and the guards' dining room made up the second floor. The Death house was torn down in 1969. You can still visit the site for your investigation. Step outside of the North Hall area and enter into the enclosed basketball court area. You will see a fence topped with razor wire encircling the area. You are now standing where the Death House once stood. This is a great place to investigate with multiple EVPS recorded at this site and feeling of static electricity by many investigators.

Photo from the Author's collection 2012

The following is a list of executions completed at the Pen. This list can help ensure you have names and dates to help in your recording of Electronic Voice Phenomena. The more accurate facts and documented information you have to aide your investigation, the better! (see the chapter on EVP for more information on how to capture these voices)

Shep Caldwell
Number: 3745
County: McDowell
Age: 25
Race: Black
Crime: Murder
Sentencing Date: August 4, 1899
Execution Date: October 10, 1899
Time Awaiting Execution: 2 months, 6 days

Frank Broadenax
Number: 3746
County: McDowell
Age: 29
Race: Black
Crime: Murder
Sentencing Date: August 5, 1899
Execution Date: November 9, 1899
Time Awaiting Execution: 2 months, 4 days

Frank Walker
Number: 3772
County: Fayette
Race: White
Crime: Murder
Sentencing Date: October 26, 1899
Execution Date: December 15, 1899
Time Awaiting Execution: 1 month, 19 days

George Carter
Number: 3972
County: Kanawha
Age: 42
Race: Black
Crime: Murder
Sentencing Date: January 19, 1901

Execution Date: March 2, 1902
Time Awaiting Execution: 1 year, 1 month, 11 days

Lewis Young
Number: 4276
County: McDowell
Age: 31
Race: Black
Crime: Murder
Sentencing Date: February 7, 1902
Execution Date: May 1, 1902
Time Awaiting Execution: 2 months, 24 days

John Mooney
Number: 4207
County: Ohio
Age: 35
Race: White
Crime: Murder
Sentencing Date: November 12, 1901
Execution Date: May 9, 1902
Time Awaiting Execution: 5 months, 27 days

Frank Friday
Number: 4208
County: Ohio
Age: 48
Race: White
Crime: Murder
Sentencing Date: November 12, 1901
Execution Date: May 9, 1902
Time Awaiting Execution: 5 months, 27 days

Perry Christian
Number: 4250
County: Fayette

Age: 31
Race: White
Crime: Murder
Sentencing Date: February 3, 1902
Execution Date: June 13, 1902
Time Awaiting Execution: 4 months, 10 days

State Henry
Number: 4100
County: Wetzel
Age: 22
Race: Black
Crime: Murder
Sentencing Date: June 14, 1901
Execution Date: October 24, 1902
Time Awaiting Execution: 1 year, 4 months, 10 days

Wilfred Davis
Number: 4307
County: Randolph
Age: 21
Race: White
Crime: Murder
Sentencing Date: May 8, 1902
Execution Date: June 5, 1903
Time Awaiting Execution: 1 year, 28 days

George Williams
Number: 5048
County: Jefferson
Age: 21
Race: Black
Crime: Rape
Sentencing Date: September 2, 1904
Execution Date: September 9, 1904
Time Awaiting Execution: 1 month, 7 days

Frank Johnson
Number: 6421
County: Harrison
Age: 34
Race: Black
Crime: Murder
Sentencing Date: June 2, 1908
Execution Date: July 17, 1908
Time Awaiting Execution: 1 month, 15 days

Arthur Brown
Number: 6806
County: McDowell
Age: 21
Race: Black
Crime: Murder
Sentencing Date: May 5, 1909
Execution Date: August 27, 1909
Time Awaiting Execution: 3 months, 22 days

Thomas Wayne
Number: 7388
County: Fayette
Age: 33
Race: Black
Crime: Murder
Sentencing Date: October 21, 1910
Execution Date: December 23, 1910
Time Awaiting Execution: 2 months, 1 day

Frank Stevenson
Number: 6125
County: Mercer
Age: 27
Race: Black

Crime: Murder
Sentencing Date: August 1, 1907
Execution Date: February 17, 1911
Time Awaiting Execution: 3 years, 6 months, 19 days

Jesse Cook
Number: 7499
County: McDowell
Age: 24
Race: White
Crime: Murder
Sentencing Date: January 27, 1911
Execution Date: March 10, 1911
Time Awaiting Execution: 1 month, 14 days

William Furbish
Number: 7528
County: Harrison
Age: 28
Race: Black
Crime: Rape
Sentencing Date: February 11, 1911
Execution Date: March 17, 1911
Time Awaiting Execution: 1 month, 6 days

James Williams
Number: 8336
County: McDowell
Age: 22
Race: Black
Crime: Murder
Sentencing Date: February 7, 1913
Execution Date: April 4, 1913
Time Awaiting Execution: 1 month, 28 days

John Marshall
Number: 8349
County: McDowell
Age: 19
Race: Black
Crime: Murder
Sentencing Date: February 7, 1913
Execution Date: April 4, 1913
Time Awaiting Execution: 1 month, 28 days

Henry Sterling
Number: 8341
County: McDowell
Age: 22
Race: Black
Crime: Murder
Sentencing Date: February 10, 1913
Execution Date: April 11, 1913
Time Awaiting Execution: 2 months, 1 day

John Hix
Number: 8356
County: McDowell
Age: 26
Race: White
Crime: Murder
Sentencing Date: February 8, 1913
Execution Date: June 6, 1913
Time Awaiting Execution: 3 months, 29 days

Henry Green
Number: 8659
County: Mingo
Age: 22
Race: Black
Crime: Murder

Sentencing Date: November 22, 1913
Execution Date: March 6, 1914
Time Awaiting Execution: 3 months, 12 days

Silas Jones
Number: 8858
County: Cabell
Age: 25
Race: Black
Crime: Murder
Sentencing Date: March 2, 1914
Execution Date: July 10, 1914
Time Awaiting Execution: 4 months, 8 days

Will Stewart
Number: 9247
County: Greenbrier
Age: 37
Race: Black
Crime: Murder
Sentencing Date: April 30, 1915
Execution Date: July 2, 1915
Time Awaiting Execution: 2 months, 2 days

Thomas Will
Number: 9294
County: Ohio
Age: 41
Race: Black
Crime: Murder
Sentencing Date: April 3, 1915
Execution Date: July 2, 1915
Time Awaiting Execution: 2 months, 29 days

Mat Jarrell
Number: 9290

County: Kanawha
Age: 24
Race: White
Crime: Murder
Sentencing Date: March 22, 1915
Execution Date: July 9, 1915
Time Awaiting Execution: 3 months, 17 days

Charles Forest
Number: 9381
County: McDowell
Age: 36
Race: Black
Crime: Murder
Sentencing Date: July 27, 1915
Execution Date: September 10, 1915
Time Awaiting Execution: 1 month, 13 days

William Sutton
Number: 9600
County: Randolph
Age: 24
Race: White
Crime: Murder
Sentencing Date: March 15, 1916
Execution Date: August 4, 1916
Time Awaiting Execution: 19 days

James Lay
Number: 9681
County: McDowell
Age: 25
Race: Black
Crime: Murder
Sentencing Date: July 12, 1916
Execution Date: September 1, 1916

Time Awaiting Execution: 1 month, 8 days

Hugh Ferguson
Number: 10614
County: Morgan
Age: 24
Race: Black
Crime: Murder
Sentencing Date: June 25, 1919
Execution Date: August 6, 1919
Time Awaiting Execution: 1 month, 12 days

Hugh Bragg
Number: 10862
County: Webster
Age: 21
Race: White
Crime: Murder
Sentencing Date: January 27, 1920
Execution Date: April 30, 1920
Time Awaiting Execution: 3 months, 3 days

Jacob Lutz
Number: 10500
County: Taylor
Age: 47
Race: White
Crime: Murder
Sentencing Date: February 16, 1920
Execution Date: July 22, 1921
Time Awaiting Execution: 1 year, 5 months, 6 days

Hobart Grimm
Number: 11320
County: Brooke
Age: 22

Race: White
Crime: Murder
Sentencing Date: April 6, 1921
Execution Date: August 5, 1921
Time Awaiting Execution: 3 months, 29 days

Henry Harbor
Number: 11556
County: McDowell
Age: 21
Race: Black
Crime: Murder
Sentencing Date: July 25, 1921
Execution Date: October 7, 1921
Time Awaiting Execution: 2 months, 13 days

Leroy Williams
Number: 11877
County: Kanawha
Age: 24
Race: Black
Crime: Rape
Sentencing Date: December 23, 1921
Execution Date: March 3, 1922
Time Awaiting Execution: 1 month, 10 days

Monroe Peyton
Number: 12085
County: Berkeley
Age: 49
Race: Black
Crime: Rape
Sentencing Date: March 14, 1922
Execution Date: May 4, 1922
Time Awaiting Execution: 1 month, 20 days

George Barrage
Number: 13227
County: Brooke
Age: 39
Race: White
Crime: Murder
Sentencing Date: July 31, 1923
Execution Date: November 2, 1923
Time Awaiting Execution: 3 months, 2 days

Dick Ferri
Number: 12987
County: Harrison
Age: 26
Race: White
Crime: Murder
Sentencing Date: April 21, 1923
Execution Date: January 4, 1924
Time Awaiting Execution: 8 months, 14 days

Philip Connizzaro
Number: 12989
County: Harrison
Age: 26
Race: White
Crime: Murder
Sentencing Date: April 21, 1923
Execution Date: January 4, 1924
Time Awaiting Execution: 8 months, 14 days

Nick Salanante
Number: 12988
County: Harrison
Age: 33
Race: White
Crime: Murder

Sentencing Date: April 14, 1923
Execution Date: January 4, 1924
Time Awaiting Execution: 8 months, 18 days

Sam Murtore
Number: 12994
County: Harrison
Age: 44
Race: White
Crime: Murder
Sentencing Date: December 7, 1923
Execution Date: February 15, 1924
Time Awaiting Execution: 2 months, 9 days

Tiny McCoy
Number: 13844
County: Pocahontas
Age: 23
Race: White
Crime: Murder
Sentencing Date: June 12, 1924
Execution Date: September 12, 1924
Time Awaiting Execution: 3 months

Robert Ford
Number: 14707
County: Harrison
Age: 24
Race: Black
Crime: Murder
Sentencing Date: June 30, 1925
Execution Date: January 29, 1926
Time Awaiting Execution: 6 months, 29 days

Henry Sawyer
Number: 15287

County: Mingo
Age: 24
Race: Black
Crime: Rape
Sentencing Date: March 17, 1926
Execution Date: April 19, 1926
Time Awaiting Execution: 1 month, 2 days

Philip Euman
Number: 15512
County: Harrison
Age: 18
Race: Black
Crime: Murder
Sentencing Date: June 22, 1926
Execution Date: August 20, 1926
Time Awaiting Execution: 1 month, 29 days

Henry Jackson
Number: 14949
County: Marshall
Age: 44
Race: Black
Crime: Murder
Sentencing Date: October 8, 1925
Execution Date: September 10, 1926
Time Awaiting Execution: 11 months, 2 days

Pierce Jeffries
Number: 15898
County: Greenbrier
Age: 21
Race: Black
Crime: Rape
Sentencing Date: November 23, 1926

Execution Date: February 18, 1927
Time Awaiting Execution: 2 months, 25 days

Wesley H. Swain
Number: 16618
County: Wood
Age: 42
Race: White
Crime: Rape
Sentencing Date: November 12, 1927
Execution Date: February 3, 1928
Time Awaiting Execution: 2 months, 21 days

Andrew Brady
Number: 15648
County: Hardy
Age: 26
Race: Black
Crime: Rape
Sentencing Date: September 7, 1926
Execution Date: March 30, 1928
Time Awaiting Execution: 1 year, 6 months, 21 days

Lawrence Fike
Number: 17299
County: Preston
Age: 24
Race: White
Crime: Murder
Sentencing Date: June 22, 1928
Execution Date: August 10, 1928
Time Awaiting Execution: 1 month, 19 days

Henry Brogan
Number: 17222
County: Raleigh

Race: Black
Crime: Rape
Sentencing Date: May 16, 1928
Execution Date: February 8, 1929
Time Awaiting Execution: 8 months, 22 days

Theodore Carr
Number: 18159
County: Pocahontas
Age: 50
Race: White
Crime: Murder
Sentencing Date: March 18, 1929
Execution Date: June 14, 1929
Time Awaiting Execution: 2 months, 27 days

Millard Morrison
Number: 18197
County: Kanawha
Age: 23
Race: White
Crime: Murder
Sentencing Date: June 3, 1929
Execution Date: September 13, 1929
Time Awaiting Execution: 3 months, 10 days

Walter Wilmot
Number: 18198
County: Kanawha
Age: 22
Race: White
Crime: Murder
Sentencing Date: June 6, 1929
Execution Date: September 13, 1929
Time Awaiting Execution: 3 months, 7 days

Execution Date: February 18, 1927
Time Awaiting Execution: 2 months, 25 days

Wesley H. Swain
Number: 16618
County: Wood
Age: 42
Race: White
Crime: Rape
Sentencing Date: November 12, 1927
Execution Date: February 3, 1928
Time Awaiting Execution: 2 months, 21 days

Andrew Brady
Number: 15648
County: Hardy
Age: 26
Race: Black
Crime: Rape
Sentencing Date: September 7, 1926
Execution Date: March 30, 1928
Time Awaiting Execution: 1 year, 6 months, 21 days

Lawrence Fike
Number: 17299
County: Preston
Age: 24
Race: White
Crime: Murder
Sentencing Date: June 22, 1928
Execution Date: August 10, 1928
Time Awaiting Execution: 1 month, 19 days

Henry Brogan
Number: 17222
County: Raleigh

Race: Black
Crime: Rape
Sentencing Date: May 16, 1928
Execution Date: February 8, 1929
Time Awaiting Execution: 8 months, 22 days

Theodore Carr
Number: 18159
County: Pocahontas
Age: 50
Race: White
Crime: Murder
Sentencing Date: March 18, 1929
Execution Date: June 14, 1929
Time Awaiting Execution: 2 months, 27 days

Millard Morrison
Number: 18197
County: Kanawha
Age: 23
Race: White
Crime: Murder
Sentencing Date: June 3, 1929
Execution Date: September 13, 1929
Time Awaiting Execution: 3 months, 10 days

Walter Wilmot
Number: 18198
County: Kanawha
Age: 22
Race: White
Crime: Murder
Sentencing Date: June 6, 1929
Execution Date: September 13, 1929
Time Awaiting Execution: 3 months, 7 days

Walter Crabtree
Number: 19056
County: Hampshire
Age: 37
Race: White
Crime: Murder
Sentencing Date: March 15, 1930
Execution Date: May 9, 1930
Time Awaiting Execution: 1 month, 24 days

Rosevelt Darnell
Number: 19630
County: Greenbrier
Age: 23
Race: White
Crime: Murder
Sentencing Date: August 8, 1930
Execution Date: November 14, 1930
Time Awaiting Execution: 3 months, 6 days

Emery Stephens
Number: 19758
County: Mingo
Age:
Race: White
Crime: Murder
Sentencing Date: November 7, 1930
Execution Date: February 20, 1931
Time Awaiting Execution: 3 months, 13 days

Will Adams
Number: 19757
County: Mingo
Age: 40
Race: White
Crime: Murder

Sentencing Date: November 6, 1930
Execution Date: February 20, 1931
Time Awaiting Execution: 3 months, 14 days

Frank Hyer
Number: 20377
County: Pocahontas
Age: 54
Race: White
Crime: Murder
Sentencing Date: March 13, 1931
Execution Date: June 19, 1931
Time Awaiting Execution: 3 months, 6 days

Harry Powers
Number: 21649
County: Harrison
Age: 39
Race: White
Crime: Murder
Sentencing Date: December 12, 1931
Execution Date: March 18, 1932
Time Awaiting Execution: 3 months, 6 days

James Blount
Number: 21886
County: Greenbrier
Age: 32
Race: Black
Crime: Murder
Sentencing Date: February 4, 1932
Execution Date: May 13, 1932
Time Awaiting Execution: 3 months, 9 days

Omer Brill
Number: 23526

County: Hardy
Age: 21
Race: White
Crime: Murder
Sentencing Date: June 30, 1933
Execution Date: August 10, 1933
Time Awaiting Execution: 1 month, 11 days

Leo Fraser
Number: 23660
County: Jackson
Age: 30
Race: White
Crime: Murder
Sentencing Date: August 19, 1933
Execution Date: November 24, 1933
Time Awaiting Execution: 3 months, 5 days

Joe Corey
Number: 23444
County: Kanawha
Age: 43
Race: White
Crime: Murder
Sentencing Date: March 11, 1933
Execution Date: December 8, 1933
Time Awaiting Execution: 8 months, 27 days

Greely Blankenship
Number: 24958
County: Mingo
Age: 29
Race: White
Crime: Murder
Sentencing Date: October 15, 1934
Execution Date: January 7, 1935

Time Awaiting Execution: 2 months, 23 days

Robert Branch
Number: 25496
County: Ohio
Age: 42
Race: Black
Crime: Murder
Sentencing Date: April 20, 1935
Execution Date: January 19, 1935
Time Awaiting Execution: 8 months, 29 days

Frank Pramesa
Number: 27172
County: Brooke
Age: 26
Race: White
Crime: Murder
Sentencing Date: November 12, 1936
Execution Date: April 13, 1937
Time Awaiting Execution: 5 months, 1 day

Willie Beckner
Number: 27685
County: Kanawha
Age: 39
Race: White
Crime: Murder
Sentencing Date: April 27, 1937
Execution Date: June 25, 1937
Time Awaiting Execution: 1 month, 28 days

Mervin Brown
Number: 28045
County: Mercer
Age: 28

Race: Black
Crime: Murder
Sentencing Date: July 29, 1937
Execution Date: September 10, 1937
Time Awaiting Execution: 1 month, 10 days

William B. Read
Number: 27536
County: Braxton
Age: 25
Race: White
Crime: Murder
Sentencing Date: January 6, 1937
Execution Date: November 5, 1937
Time Awaiting Execution: 6 months, 29 days

Arnett A. Booth
Number: 28256
County: Cabell
Age: 47
Race: White
Crime: Kidnap
Sentencing Date: December 11, 1937
Execution Date: March 21, 1938
Time Awaiting Execution: 3 months, 10 days

John Travis
Number: 28257
County: Cabell
Age: 25
Race: White
Crime: Kidnap
Sentencing Date: December 13, 1937
Execution Date: March 21, 1938
Time Awaiting Execution: 3 months, 8 days

Orville Adkins
Number: 28258
County: Cabell
Age: 25
Race: White
Crime: Kidnap
Sentencing Date: December 17, 1937
Execution Date: March 21, 1938
Time Awaiting Execution: 3 months, 4 days

Raymond Styres
Number: 27499
County: Ohio
Age: 28
Race: White
Crime: Murder
Sentencing Date: March 31, 1938
Execution Date: March 13, 1939
Time Awaiting Execution: 11 months, 10 days

Byzantine Hartman
Number: 30929
County: Upshur
Age: 29
Race: White
Crime: Murder
Sentencing Date: May 16, 1940
Execution Date: June 28, 1940
Time Awaiting Execution: 1 month, 12 days

Paul Tross
Number: 30940
County: Mineral
Age: 40
Race: Black
Crime: Murder

Sentencing Date: June 11, 1940
Execution Date: December 6, 1940
Time Awaiting Execution: 5 months, 24 days

James Chambers
Number: 26339
County: Randolph
Age: 23
Race: Black
Crime: Murder
Sentencing Date: February 21, 1945
Execution Date: March 30, 1945
Time Awaiting Execution: 1 month, 7 days

William Turner
Number: 33831
County: Preston
Age: 27
Race: White
Crime: Murder
Sentencing Date: November 3, 1945
Execution Date: December 28, 1945
Time Awaiting Execution: 1 month, 25 days

Richard Collins
Number: 34138
County: Kanawha
Age: 22
Race: White
Crime: Murder
Sentencing Date: May 15, 1946
Execution Date: October 11, 1946
Time Awaiting Execution: 1 month, 26 days

William Gordon
Number: 34212

County: Mercer
Age: 20
Race: White
Crime: Murder
Sentencing Date: August 16, 1946
Execution Date: January 3, 1947
Time Awaiting Execution: 1 month, 18 days

Paul W. Burton
Number: 35040
County: Logan
Age: 33
Race: White
Crime: Murder
Sentencing Date: October 18, 1947
Execution Date: January 2, 1948
Time Awaiting Execution: 2 months, 15 days

Mark McCauley
Number: 34348
County: Mineral
Age: 35
Race: White
Crime: Murder
Sentencing Date: November 18, 1946
Execution Date: January 30, 1948
Time Awaiting Execution: 1 year, 2 months, 12 days

Mathew Perison
Number: 35482
County: Logan
Age: 31
Race: Black
Crime: Murder
Sentencing Date: July 7, 1948
Execution Date: September 23, 1948

Time Awaiting Execution: 2 months, 16 days

Lemuel Steed
Number: 35557
County: Fayette
Age: 28
Race: Black
Crime: Murder
Sentencing Date: August 9, 1948
Execution Date: October 15, 1948
Time Awaiting Execution: 2 months, 6 days

Bud Peterson
Number: 35825
County: Logan
Age: 56
Race: Black
Crime: Murder
Sentencing Date: January 14, 1949
Execution Date: February 25, 1949
Time Awaiting Execution: 1 month, 11 days

Fred Painter
Number: 37480
County: Kanawha
Age: 31
Race: White
Crime: Murder
Execution Date: March 26, 1951
Time Awaiting Execution: 1 month, 11 days
Method of Execution: Electrocution
Harry Burdette
Number: 37481
County: Kanawha
Age: 21
Race: White

Crime: Murder
Execution Date: March 26, 1951
Time Awaiting Execution: 1 month, 11 days
Method of Execution: Electrocution

James Hewlett
Number: 37398
County: Cabell
Age: 22
Race: White
Crime: Murder
Execution Date: April 10, 1951
Time Awaiting Execution: 3 months
Method of Execution: Electrocution

Oschel Gardner
Number: 38742
County: Mason
Age: 22
Race: White
Crime: Murder
Execution Date: April 17, 1953
Time Awaiting Execution: 2 months, 3 days
Method of Execution: Electrocution

Tom Ingram
Number: 39207
County: McDowell
Age: 32
Race: Black
Crime: Murder
Execution Date: March 27, 1954
Time Awaiting Execution: 4 months, 7 days
Method of Execution: Electrocution

Robert Hopkins
Number: 40669
County: Kanawha
Age: 27
Race: White
Crime: Murder
Execution Date: September 7, 1956
Time Awaiting Execution: 3 months, 28 days
Method of Execution: Electrocution

Eugene Linger
Number: 41432
County: Upshur
Age: 29
Race: White
Crime: Murder
Execution Date: June 5, 1958
Time Awaiting Execution: 7 months, 9 days
Method of Execution: Electrocution

Larry Paul Fudge
Number: 41721
County: Cabell
Age: 25
Race: White
Crime: Murder
Execution Date: July 1, 1958
Time Awaiting Execution: 3 months, 2 days
Method of Execution: Electrocution

Elmer D. Bruner
Number: 41334
County: Cabell
Age: 41
Race: White
Crime: Murder

Execution Date: April 3, 1959
Time Awaiting Execution: 1 year, 7 months, 25 days
Method of Execution: Electrocution

Whitegate cemetery in Moundsville
Photo by Author

The electric chair that was used at the West Virginia Pen is an impressive piece of oak furniture and sits solemnly in the lobby of the building greeting visitors as they walks through the heavy front door. It was partially built by an inmate by the name of Paul Glenn. He was the head carpenter for the job. As the story goes, Glenn needed to be removed from the general population after the chair was completed due to inmate threats.

On March 26, 1951, Fred Painter and Harry Burdette, both convicted of murdering Edward C. O'Brien, were the first inmates to be put to death by electrocution at the West Virginia Penitentiary. The two had been convicted of kicking a soft drink salesman to death in a parking lot on the corner of Washington and Summers streets in downtown

Charleston, West Virginia. Painter had to be jolted twice after two physicians found that he was still alive after the first round. Painter was pronounced dead more than nine minutes after sitting in the chair. It took a little more than three minutes worth of electricity to execute Burdette.

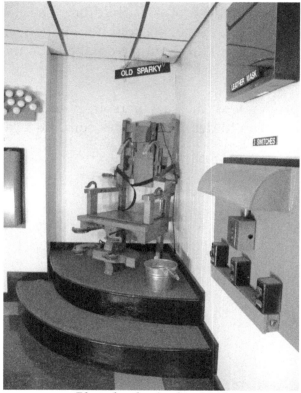

Photo by the Author 2012

The last execution performed at the Pen was 43 year old Elmer Bruner. Elmer was convicted of murder, but pleaded his innocence until the end. On April 3rd 1959, Elmer enjoyed his last meal. Ham, mashed potatoes and gravy, jello, garden salad, biscuits, peaches and coffee. Afterwards, he took a nap and later that evening, walked the final steps towards the solid oak chair made for death. A hood was placed upon his head and 18 onlookers watched in attention as shocks of 1700 volts and two 500 volts hit the inmate. He was pronounced dead just eight minutes later.

His family learned of his execution by radio at their home in Huntington. They were too poor to afford a trip to visit him. What a sad event for such a hard working family. Elmer was the second oldest of six children. The family was struggling and the father of six sold newspapers and pencils on a street corner in Huntington to make ends meet, which they rarely did.

Elmer Bruner was the last person in the state of West Virginia to be put to death for crimes committed at the state penitentiary.

CHAPTER 4
STAFF & VOLUNTEER GHOST SIGHTINGS

Lori O'Neil has been a familiar face at the WV Pen for many years. Lori can be found leading ghost tours at night, selling items at the gift shop, organizing the local Zombie Walk, and working on the Halloween haunted house at the Pen each October called the Dungeon of Terrors. She is one busy lady! She has led just about every tour for us on our private ghostly over nighters at the WV Pen. During the last several years I have seen her answer both historical and paranormal questions about the Pen and she has been featured on quite a few off the paranormal television shows. Due to her knowledge and experience at the Pen, she is a valuable asset and full of stories! Lori lives in Moundsville and is not with an organized ghost hunting group...but that doesn't mean she hasn't had any experiences! I asked her what drew her to the Pen in the first place. Lori said, "I'm from Moundsville and have always been fascinated with the building. After I came to work here, I listened to all of the paranormal stories with interest and started researching it."

When asked what areas of the Pen could be the most paranormally active, Lori had this answer, "I have believed that with all of the violence that occurred in the Penitentiary, there has to be activity throughout. I do believe in the paranormal. I have seen an apparition while in the Sugar Shack area and I was with my husband, Elza O'Neil. I have recorder EVPs and I have seen shadow people several times. My favorite equipment to work with is the basic, a camera and a voice recorder."

I asked Lori due to her being in the Pen on thousands of occasions, what paranormal event stands out in her memory. Lori told me this, "While in the Sugar Shack, a group of people walked by me. One man left the group and walked back over towards me. He was approximately six feet tall and right in front of me. I spoke to him. He disappeared right in front of me!"

Steve Hummel is the owner of Steve's Gym and Fitness. He has been an investigator of the paranormal for almost 6 years and has worked the haunted house every October at the Pen for the last 11 years. He states that his first impression of the Pen was that he was drawn to it but yet at times, and in some areas, has feelings of fear. (He is not alone!) On Steve's feeling about the Pen, Steve adds, "I would be honest and say that it depressed and also expressed every emotion for me. Every visit and every tour is an experience there for me. I couldn't count how many times I've been within the walls. I have been involved in many ghost hunts there and throughout the other states. I am a member of a paranormal group called Mountaineer Paranormal. I am also involved on a television project called Paranormal Quest."
http://www.youtube.com/ParanormalQuestDRS. There is also a personal paranormal project I'm working on called EPS, which is a convention to bring together groups and promote unity with them. You can also check out http://archive-afterlife.weebly.com/

I asked Steve if he thought he was a bit sensitive to the paranormal and what his paranormal experiences were on site, if any. Steve said, "I am a sensitive and I have had a lot of paranormal experiences at the West Virginia state prison. The list of experiences is as vast as it is long. I have had physical experiences which range from being pushed to having my hand grasped. I feel far more spiritual experiences than physical. Oppression seems to be the key preference of what the spirits use to communicate there. I have seen three shadow people in my time working there. I have also heard footsteps cell doors opening and closing and have seen and heard objects moved. I have seen flashlights being turned on and off, along with unexplained cold spots and disembodied voices." Steve continues, "My favorite place to investigate would definitely be the "original" lock-up area, which is where "honor hall" was at the closing of the institution. That area is far more oppressive than anywhere else I've investigated. I would've said the "original" administrative building, but I have only walked through it a few times." I asked Steve what kind of gear he preferred to use and he said, "I'm not a big fan of carrying bunch equipment, too much noise and effort. Simplicity!! I prefer a digital voice recorder with/ MCOMM, flashlight and Handicam or camera."

Maggie Gray is a retired Correctional Officer and Trainer who lives in Cameron, West Virginia. She started at the West Virginia Pen in 1987 as a Correctional Officer and currently, she is a tour guide on site and works as one of the gift shop Clerks. When Maggie saw the Pen for the first time she thought "This is amazing. This is what I should have been doing all my adult life." What drew her to take a job with the state? Insurance!

Maggie does not belong to a paranormal organization or group. She doesn't think that she is overly sensitive or even psychic but has had some unexplainable instances of the paranormal while at the building. Maggie says "I've seen something and have heard an inmate who was murdered in prison say my name. He, or something, ran something across the back of my neck when I asked if he would let me know if he were there with me. Very creepy!!"

Does Maggie believe in the paranormal? She says, "I believe that something ...lost souls... if you will, linger there when they die." What do you think is the most "active" area of the Pen? Maggie says, "At any given time every place in the prison is active. Some areas more than others, but I wouldn't count any place in the prison as in-active. In my opinion, the most active areas are North Hall, front lobby and the Museum. "

I asked Maggie about those experiences and what had happened at that time? Maggie relates,"Red Snyder said "Mornin' Mag." I answered saying, "Mornin' Red," just as I did every time I went by his cell. I was the only one in the prison at that time. This took place about 9:30 a.m. in June of 2006 or 2007. I also had gone to North Hall to do an EVP session with Polly Gear. I told (the spirit) Red that the man who murdered him was released from prison. On the tape you could hear very clearly, "I ALREADY KNOW." I then asked if he would give me some sort of sign that he was there and a couple of seconds later I felt what felt like a finger ran across the back of my neck. Very creepy and I left the hall immediately. Maggie speaks of the infamous Shadow Man, "In the Lobby the form of a man (Shadow Man) walked right across the room. There were two other people who saw it at the same time. The figure was very tall and you could actually see it taking steps, although it had no feet. This happened in October of 2009."

Many people don't think of the museum area as a haunted spot. Very few people realize that when TAPS Ghosthunters filmed several years ago, they checked out the Museum area and were intrigued by it; it just never made the final edit. Maggie tells us, "In the Museum, a door which never opens flew open and banged against a display case. A couple of seconds later a very cold gush of air swirled around my feet and legs. A couple of seconds after that the door almost closed again on its own. This happened in July 2006."

Museums are great places to investigate due to the energy of the items. This museum also happens to be the area where "Old Sparky" is on display along with many various homemade weapons confiscated at the Pen during its 129 year history.

Ryan Zacheri is from the Moundsville area and spends as much time as he can in helping to lead some tours at the Pen. Ryan loves to investigate and has a knack for video editing which can come in handy! He says this, "Finding proof of an afterlife has become my life's passion and I figured what better way to share that with the world than with the world of television. It is with this thought that my best friends and I created "Paranormal Quest."This paranormal documentary show chronicles me and my two best friends Dave and Steve as we search for paranormal activity. I am very experienced in shooting and editing video, and use that talent to the fullest. My life will always be a mystery just like the activity I chase."

Polly Gear lives in Clarksburg, West Virginia. She has the enviable position as a paranormal guide at the public ghost hunts. She has been investigating for eleven years and is the founder and investigator for Mountaineer Paranormal. www.mountaineerparanormal.ning.com

Mountaineer Paranormal was created in 1999 in Clarksburg. This is a team of dedicated people who wish to learn and study about paranormal or spirit activity, as their website states.

Polly says her first visit to the Pen was in 1997 and that she has been there over one hundred times for both ghost hunts and day tours. Polly also says she is sensitive to activity and can see, feel, and hear them. When asked what she thought of the old prison the first time she saw it she said,"I was impressed...felt some fear but felt more excitement. I started going to the Pen not long after it closed. They were giving a Saturday night mini tour for ten dollars for a few hours. I have been hooked ever since. I definitely believe in the paranormal and think the Pen is haunted without a doubt. When asked what she believes to be the most active areas of the building she offers this, "From my experiences investigating at the Pen, I have found that the activity inside seems to travel from area to area and year to year. In earlier years, the most active areas were the Sugar Shack, the south basement area and the North Hall cell block. In the last few years it was the Shadow man hallway and New Wall cell block. At the present we find that the medical infirmary and kitchen areas are most active."

Polly says, "My favorite part about paranormal investigating is recording EVP so I guess my favorite piece of equipment is a digital voice recorder." With so many visits to the West Virginia Pen, Polly has had many experiences. She says, "I have had quite a few in many areas of the prison, such as having my hair tugged and physically touched while sitting at the tables in the North Hall cell block. I have heard men crying and moaning in the Infirmary and Psych Ward areas. A friend and I have witnessed a headless man walk through the hallway wall into one of the psych cells that are locked. I have captured on video, in the psych ward the voice of someone saying my name and me answering it without realizing I was in the area alone at the time. I have had an audible voice answer to a question asked out loud in the New Wall cell block- after hearing shuffling above on the tier walkway, I asked "Who are you?" and a voice says " Jimmy." Then nothing more was heard.

Polly's most memorable experience to date, has been her run in and capturing on film, of the Shadow Man. Read about her experience in detail and more encounters with the Shadow Man in the chapter, The Shadow Man Cometh in the book *The Haunted History of the West Virginia Penitentiary.*

David Gear is the son of Polly Gear. He is another member of Mountaineer Paranormal and a volunteer paranormal guide at Pen ghost hunts. He is also one of the haunted house actors for the Dungeon of Horrors held every October at the prison. He is the tech manager for his investigative groups and has been investigating the paranormal for ten years so far. He has been to the prison on over three hundred occasions for day tours and night ghost hunts as well. David is a sensitive and has the ability to sense when entities are around. His favorite equipment to use on a hunt is a digital voice recorder and a camcorder.

"The first time I ever laid eyes on the penitentiary my jaw dropped." David continues, "How could this massive stone structure stay so well hidden within the city streets of a small town? It was incredible how this Gothic style building that was hell on earth for thousands of men and women could be so beautiful."

David believes the building is haunted without a doubt and is firm in his belief to the point that he offers, "If the West Virginia Penitentiary is not haunted then I no longer believe in the paranormal." David's pick for the most active location inside is the medical infirmary but had his most notable experience in the south ends basement. He explains "Back before the south end of the basement was closed off, a group of three of us were down there. My mother, Polly, another group member and I were doing an EVP session when things started to get weird. I heard my mother talking and I heard her voice begin to change. She started to sound like a man while she was doing EVP. At the same time I could hear our other member talking as well but they sounded normal. I looked over at my mom and her face looked like a man that I have never seen before. At that point I suggested that we wrap up the EVP session and we left. This was the most extraordinary thing I've ever witnessed at the penitentiary."

CHAPTER 5
PARANORMAL ENCOUNTERS

Jodi Ivy hails from Doylestown, Ohio and has been to the Pen more times than she can remember. She's a nursing student, a wife and mom but ghost hunting is a passion she has had for awhile. Jodi is an Empath and Paranormal Investigator. She has also helped out Haunted Heartland Tours as one of the Skeleton Crew members for a few years. Jodi states, "I have been to prison more times than I'd like to admit! For whatever reason, I am drawn to the Pen. It's one of my favorite places to haunt. I have had numerous experiences at the Pen so I will narrow it down to the two most memorable ones for me. I was in the infirmary/psychiatric ward and kept hearing sounds like someone was banging a metal food tray on the table. Then all the sudden I feel a pull on the back of my shirt - turned around and nothing was there. A few minutes later, I kept hearing voices and hearing sounds like water running coming from the room where the ice-baths took place to calm aggressive prisoners. Well the only place in the prison that has running water is the main lobby!"

Jodi continues, "My other memorable experience was down in the Boiler Room, aka, "the Hole" where R.D. Wall was murdered. I am always intrigued to go and sit down there alone and each time I do, I experience something either it by EVP, feeling of anxiousness or pictures. I remember one time in particular that I had been sitting down there alone, and I kept feeling really irritated and bothered for some reason - at that moment I took a picture and in the picture there is an unexplained mist surrounding the chair in front of me. I also have gotten EVPs one of which is a disturbing voice of a scared distraught man yelling, "let me out" - there was no body down there except me! I believe that the Pen is haunted by the past prisoners due to the amount of death that took place in the prison walls. It is also said that if you die in prison, your soul remains there - I am a firm believer in that."

Boiler room mist
Photo by Jodi Ivy

Jodi continues with her experiences at the Pen, "I have had numerous experiences at Moundsville Pen. It is one of my favorite places to hunt. During one of our tours (I believe it was April 2010, the dates all run together after you've been there so many times) we were doing the usual informational walk around tour with Lori O'Neil. We were in the "bullpen" area of Maximum Security rounding people up. Mind you there were 40+ people there on that hunt. We usually let people wander down the cell-block near Danny Lehman's (he had been murdered with an ice pick type tool to the eye) cell which is the first cell at the beginning of the block. Forty plus people had already walked through the area and back up through again. Well... I walked down the cell block to gather up the stragglers and as I walked back up behind the tour crowd, I walked by Danny's cell and felt like cobwebs had gotten all over me - which is impossible due to the fact that 40+ people including myself had walked through that area twice - if it had been cobwebs they would have been cleared away by all those people. Many of us ghost fanatics know the story behind the cobweb affect.

For those of you who don't, please allow me to explain the theory of the cobweb affect. ECTOPLASM: The substance left behind when an entity tries to manifest itself. Although still largely theoretical (none has yet been collected for chemical analysis) it has been photographed on many occasions. Ectoplasm often appears as a thick white mist or smoke in nearly straight lines. Vapor and humidity is often mistaken for is often mistaken for ectoplasm. It is rarely seen with the naked eye. It can, however, be felt as a dense area of cobweb-like strands. Some say too that you will get that cobweb feeling when you are in a "charged" area. As usual I did not have my camera with me at the time. Had I had it with me, then maybe I would have caught a glimpse of Danny Lehman."

Karen Dillenger came on a ghost hunt one night a few years ago. This is her story. "I drove up from southern Virginia and came up to do this ghost hunt I had seen advertised online. I knew I didn't want to do a big public ghost hunt and this sounded like it would be right up my alley. I had a cousin of mine who lived in West Virginia a long time ago and he was a prisoner here so I was really excited about having a family connection. I walked by myself after the tour was over. I know you are not supposed to do that but I really wanted to be alone. I knew that my cousin had been in South Hall, but I did not know which cell. He was only there for a few years and then was paroled. My mom told me he never liked to talk about those dark days and I which he had. Anyway, I ventured into South Hall, and sat down on a cold bunk...it was November and very cold I remember. I wrapped up even more in my jacket and held my recorder steady. I didn't really think I captured anything until about a week later. I played my recorder back and listened to about 30 minutes of tape. I heard nothing until the last three minutes. I rewound my tape and played it again. I distinctly hear a man laughing very low and for about 20 seconds. After that I hear a few mumbled words in the same man's voice. It sounded like he was right next to me. I was all alone. Boy, did that really freak me out!"

Louis Charles is an author and webmaster hailing from Massillon, Ohio. He is the author of "Helping Ghosts" and the owner of the website www.AngelsGhosts.com. Louis also works occasionally with a paranormal investigation group called Sight of Ohio. In his interview I asked him how many years he had been ghost hunting? Louis replied "My work in this field began in '96 in a roundabout way. 14 years I guess."

Louis made a visit to the Pen to meet up with Polly Gear, photographer of the Shadow Man photo. I asked him about that visit in 2006 and he said his first impression of the Pen was "spooky" and that he does believe the building to be haunted. Louis says, "I interviewed Polly Gear in-person around November 2006. After watching what TAPS did to Polly Gear on SciFi's Ghost Hunters, I felt compelled to contact her and debunk the TAPS debunking. I did more of more a walk-through and re-creation of Polly's photo. (See the Shadow Man Cometh chapter) We did try and record EVP in several places inside the prison (sugar shack, jail cells, etc.) I do believe in the paranormal and consider myself to be "sensitive" at times. Sometimes I can feel, and sometimes can discern messages from them, especially enlightened spirits who may be helping ghosts. My favorite equipment is experimental stuff: IR cameras, Ghost box recording, etc." When asked what area was more active, Louis says, "The kitchen area seems to be the spot to see the shadow man. I have also received another photo from someone with a walking shadow man in the kitchen."

Louis is the author of "Jesus Religion: A Critical Examination of Christian Insanity and Helping Ghosts: A Guide to Understanding Lost Spirits."Both books are available at online book sellers and thru his website at www.AngelsGhosts.com.

Andrea Albright lives in Streetsboro, Ohio where she works as a Claim Representative. This is her experience: "We went down on the bus tour with Sherri Brake to the West Virginia Pen and we were going around on the tour with the guide. While we were in the Sugar Shack I heard someone whisper my husband's name in my ear and no one was standing by me. Also, later while we were alone in the Sugar Shack with a small group I became very angry and wanted to punch the person next to me and I'm not like that.

Marc Cunningham lives in Guelph, Ontario, Canada is 42 years old and has been on a few Haunted Heartland Tours. Marc is a Nurse and for a few years he volunteered in Mansfield, Ohio at the Ohio State Reformatory as a tour guide. He is not a member of any paranormal group but has been into paranormal investigations for about eight years. He has been to the Pen three times for nighttime ghost hunting. I asked Marc to tell us a bit about his experiences at the Pen since prisons seemed to be his thing. (haha) Marc says, "Hey, I am not a medium or anything, but I do believe in the paranormal. My first impression of the pen was just a sense of being over-whelmed by this huge building. It takes up what, like an entire city block? I can't imagine what it would have been like to be sentenced to serve time at that place. It breaks your spirit just by looking at it. I went to the Pen on one of your Haunted Heartland ghost hunt tours a few years ago. I believe there is some sort of unusual activities that occur at Moundsville, I cannot say it is paranormal, nor can I say it is haunted. I personally do not have enough evidence to make that statement."

Marc enlightens us, "My event occurred by the mailroom, by that round entrance gate. (The Wheel) The person I went with had an amazing experience in the psych ward that night. The tools I use when I ghost hunt are a digital camera, an EVP meter and a digital voice recorder." Marc continues on with more of his own experience, "It really is nothing too exciting meaning no blood dripping from the walls or a full body ghost appearing in front of my face yelling "boo". Anyway, as I think back on that night, it wasn't so much one event, but a series of "things that make you go "hhhhmmmm?" I was standing by where that round entrance gate is, by the post office I think, (The Wheel) I inhaled and smelled the strongest smell of whiskey. It really was as if somebody held a bottle right under my nose. So I inhaled again to make sure I wasn't imagining it and it was gone, nothing. I thought I did imagine it until I heard a lady about ten feet behind me say to her friend "Did you just smell whiskey?" So this odor moved and it seemed to be very localized. I know you don't allow spirits of that type on your tours, and I am not a whiskey drinking guy, so where did that smell come from? My partner that night for the hunt was Iona. She and I came down from the psych ward, and she got the coolest photo in the room with the dental equipment."

Marc mentions glimpsing the shadowy figures that many people see, "We went upstairs in the psych ward I think, I can't remember what it was, but it had a lot of glass around it. Iona and I hung out there and I know I kept seeing these black shapes moving out of the corner of my right eye. It would drive me crazy because as soon as I looked over there it would be gone."

Unusual lights in the Dental Room upstairs
From the author's collection

Marc continues on, "We heard one pane of glass rattle in the window frame along that long hallway between the cafeteria and where the tours start and I know there was no wind that night, no big trucks going by, nobody walking on the floor above us. I made it a point to check all those things out and it was only one pane. We watched and listened to it rattle for about 5 minutes and then it just stopped. Never heard it rattle the rest of the night. That was my experience, I know Iona had a couple of strange things happen to her because she went out with the couple we came with, Vince and Karen, and I stayed back for coffee. I remember Iona saying her friend kept "sensing a presence" around her. And when they took pictures of her, an orange streak was around her, or beside her. Other times she said it was gone and they took pictures of her and there was no orange streak in any of the pictures."

Lisa Roark of Princeton, West Virginia is a nurse as well. Her experience at the Pen went like this, "When getting ready to exit a room myself and three friends (all females) stated "We are getting ready to leave is there anything that you would like to tell us?" On my DVR a male voice says "No- Have a nice night." There was no one else in the room with us, it was just us girls!

Tristate Paranormal Research Society checked out the Pen in 2011. The group was founded in 1994 by Debbie Fletcher and has 17 years of research and service in the paranormal field. Their team primarily responds to residential requests from families believing they are experiencing activity that is of a paranormal nature. They use scientific methods to collect and document the activity and offer counseling and resources to obtain a resolution to the activity when warranted.

Tristate investigated the Pen in 2011 and this is what they reported, "Our team arrived at the prison with our standard equipment.(digital recorders, digital cameras, emf meters, temp meters, kll meters, enhanced audio devices and camcorders. This time our "trigger objects" were two of our investigators who happen to work in law enforcement. They brought along handcuffs, key rings, nightsticks and one wore a correction officer uniform. The team accompanied a good friend and veteran investigator from California to the location where we met with other people planning to investigate the prison that night. Moods, emotions and expectations were high with our team simply do to the fact that this was going to be a "hunt" for fun. No pressure or worries and hopefully we would walk away with some awesome experiences and data."

"The building itself is rather ominous looking. The older section of the prison we were later informed, would be 'off limits to us because it was not structurally sound. Entering the facility I couldn't help but notice the horrid smell. It was not only of mold and mildew, but apparently bats had taken up residence and the odor was overpowering at times. My team was aware of the history of the location and also had inside facts due to that one of our investigators had been a corrections officer at this very prison right up until its closure. Our mindset for this location was simply this, aggravate and provoke....which we did in abundance. Beyond some modest temp fluctuations and a few EMF spikes environmentally speaking, we were unable to collect data to support or discount any of the claims. This is not to say it is not there, we were just unable to collect it at this time. The likelihood for this particular location to indeed have paranormal activity is high and I myself have reviewed evidence from other investigators that has been very interesting."

"Our review of all the data collected including audio, video and photographic yielded nothing of any note or interest. As with many locations the lack of evidence was a bit disappointing however it was a great experience investigating the location with such a strong historical significance."

Keith Harris hails from Cleveland Ohio and works in the maintenance field. He is an investigator with the Cuyahoga Paranormal Society. When asked about any experiences he had while at the Pen, he says "We were on one of the Haunted Heartland Tours about two years ago. We went down into the Sugar Shack and after taking some pictures we started doing some EVP work. WE started working with some dowsing rods which crossed very quickly each time we used them. After I gave them to my friend, to try, I was standing and behind me I felt a slight touch to my hair. Not sure if what something brushing my hair or breathing on me so I had someone check and see if there was something crawling on me. There were no cobwebs there either. I felt a cold spot happen suddenly which seemed to last about two-three minutes. My friends took a photo of me standing there and did they not catch anything unfortunately. I really enjoyed this experience as it was my first time something like this happened to me."

Sage Recco, a psychology college student at Kent State University, visited the Pen in 2006 for the first time. She has been there a total of four times since then and considers herself to be a 'little' sensitive at times. She says, "I do have the ability to feel spirits and I am able to sense when an area is being affected by a spirit." When asked what she thought about the Pen when she first glimpsed it she said, "Wow. I can't even imagine what kinds of criminals were held back by those old walls." My mother, Sherri Brake, offered me to come along and to help her for the night. I believed it would be a very interesting trip with my mom and it was definitely unforgettable!"

When asked about her belief in the paranormal Sage said, "I do believe that once people pass away they can and do leave pieces of their history and even their personalities behind. I do very much believe that the Pen is being affected, possibly haunted, from the souls of the past prisoners. I think the most active are is the Psych Ward, for sure. I had my first big EVP experience in the Medical Infirmary / Dental Room area." When asked for details she said, "I was wandering the rooms in the Medical ward and Psych ward when I came upon the dentist chair sitting in a creepy room. I felt as if the air was heavier there than in any other room I had been in that night. I decided that I would use the tape recorder and I would ask a few questions. I asked questions such as "What is your name?", "Why are you here at the West Virginia Pen?" and how they felt about us being there. Later on in the night, mom and I were driving home when we decided to play the cassette tape in our SUV. We could hear me asking, "Are you okay that we are here?" And then we listened for anything. As we strained for an answer, we heard a slightly whispered and muffled reply, "I love you" a man said. We both jumped with the excitement of the EVP recording. It was my first EVP try and I got something! We were both so excited that we had recorded an EVP. It was really cool and I was a complete skeptic!

Denise Drake is a Federal Security Officer from Akron, Ohio who has been investigating the paranormal for about many years and is a talented photographer. Denise does not belong to an organized group. Her favorite equipment to use on investigations is a "good digital camera, pendulum, and to just open myself up and use all of my senses to 'feel' around me."

She has been to the Pen on four separate occasions so far with two being overnight ghost hunts with Haunted Heartland Tours. On April 29 2007 and September 29 2007, she attended our Ghost Hunting 101 classes at the Pen which gave her the opportunity to investigate the Pen in a smaller group setting. Denise says that when she first saw the old prison, she could not believe how massive and foreboding it was. In her opinion, it's definitely an active and haunted location. The areas that Denise list's as most active are the cell tiers, Psych Ward and the cafeteria.

Denise tells us, "In the Psych Ward I picked up mostly on just feelings of depression, despair and felling of being trapped." She continues on, "During one of the ghost hunting classes, there are fewer people so you really have the place to yourself. I was venturing into an area not far from the solitary cells area (by Red Snyder's cell in North Hall) and I felt water or something being thrown on me. I had a photography vest on and could hear the droplets...whatever hitting the vest. I looked up and around...then I went and asked Sherri Brake and one of the employees if there were any water pipes or something else that could be causing that. There were none on in that section, and the windows were quite a distance away from where I was standing (besides the fact that it was not raining). Then it crossed my mind that maybe somehow 'they' could sense that I was in law enforcement, and if you have watched any television or movies, prisoners would often throw their...um...saved bodily functions and throw it at officers. I really hope that wasn't it, but I have no other explanations!"

Other locations have offered some experiences for Denise Drake as well. "I have experienced cold spots, especially in the psych ward and have taken pictures of orbs or energy balls there. (Not to mention it's just creepy up there!). I have heard noises in and around the kitchen area and have taken pictures that have had energy streaks in the hallway (same hall where the 'shadow man' picture was taken). In many areas where you walk around you will feel many emotions, they still have been held within those walls and I am sure for many years to come."

Anita Love lives in Canal Winchester, Ohio and has been to the Pen on one occasion. She works as a Police Dispatcher with the Columbus Police Department. Anita says "I went to Sherri Brakes Ghost Hunting 101 class in November of 2008 at the WV Pen and captured 2 class A EVPs. One sounds like a cell door being shaken and then a male says "whore" very clearly. The 2nd one is a male's voice whispering "some angel died." There were no other tour members around at the time we did the EVPs. Also, we got some good bright orb photos."

Tammy Ammon is a mom and paranormal investigator with a true sense of adventure. She lives in North Lawrence, Ohio and says she has been to the Pen more times than she can remember. She works for the Parks and Recreation department in Stark County and is a Paranormal Investigator with the Boo Crew PI's. He experience went like this "Dianne, Brenda and I were in Red Snyder's cell and got a blast of cold air, like someone turned on an air conditioner. A breeze went by us and we got an EVP. When we asked if Red was there and he said "Yes." We also saw a shadow in South Hall on the 2nd level. We all go in the same cell every time we come down to the Pen. Amanda has been scratched there. It is always active when we go to Moundsville. Amanda and Staci heard a radio in North Hall. There are NO radios there and no one else around. We hear whispers and see shadows each time we visit. It's an awesome place!"

Debra Robinson is a published author, psychic, and palm reader and is a professional musician. She lives in New Philadelphia, Ohio and has been to the Pen several times from 2007-2012. Her husband, Rod often accompanies her on investigation. Debra believes the building to be paranormally active, which is no surprise as she often has had experiences while there. She tells us some of the area's she is drawn to investigate in the old prison, "The first hallway after leaving the lobby area, Red Snyder's cell area, and the Alamo section in North Hall, There are just so many really awful feeling places, The atmosphere is so thick you could cut it with a knife, it's pretty brutal for anyone with any psychic ability at all...almost unbearable at times. It's the kind of place you feel oppressed, and threatened, and in danger of being attacked." Check out her website at www.psychicdebra.net

Jill Keppler is another investigator of the paranormal and lives in Parma, Ohio. She has ventured to the WV Pen many times and has lost count. She works as a Field Office Coordinator but finds time to volunteer and lead tours at the Ohio State Reformatory where she has volunteered for numerous years. She says this about her first Pen visit, "On my very first visit to the WV Pen, I was doing EVP work in the Psych Ward. I was in the far end where the small cells are located. You could tell there was someone with me, so I was looking forward to reviewing the tape. When I played the tape back the next day, there was a man's voice that distinctly said, "Don't scream." Jill is a great investigator and gets to hone her skills quite often at the Reformatory.

David Walter volunteered to let me listen to some EVP files recorded in June 2010. David told me via email, "The files are labeled and contain some great EVP's. We even get some responses to questions in the Hole and in Red Snyder's cell. The Sugar Shack recording is the one where Cheri gets pushed out of the chair and the recorder goes flying and you can hear all sorts of things while it is lying on the ground."

Robyn Kuhlbursh lives in Ohio and loves to investigate locations such as the Pen. She captured an unusual photo while on a hunt there several years ago. Robyn says "In the kitchen of the WV Pen, I captured a cool photograph. I believe it was in June of 2009. After taking the picture, my digital camera made a popping and sizzling noise and went "dead." I replaced the batteries, looked at my last picture, and realized I had something unusual!

John Kachuba is an author and certified ghost hunter living in Cincinnati, Ohio with his wife Mary. He is not a member of a ghost hunting or paranormal organization but has investigated many locations across the world. He has been investigating the paranormal for nearly 10 years and has a website (www.JohnKachuba.com) which features his upcoming presentations, events, and book tours. His books are very popular and can be purchased online at www.Amazon.com or at local bookstores.

John is the author of Ghosthunting Ohio: On the Road Again. Ghosthunters: On the Trail of Mediums, Dowsers, Spirit Seekers and Other Investigators of America's Paranormal World, Ghosthunting Illinois and Ghosthunting Ohio, How to Write Funny, The Gathering of Stones, and Why is this Job Killing Me? (Co-authored with his wife, Mary A. Newman, PhD).

John visited the West Virginia Pen in 2007 for the first time. He doesn't possess any special psychic talents or abilities but is always intrigued by others who do. I know this first hand as John and I have done a few investigations together.

Upon seeing the mammoth building for the first time, John thought it was suitably creepy! I asked him what had drawn him there for that evening and John told me " While I was teaching at Ohio University in Athens, Ohio some professors and students from the Sociology Department that were studying prisons, decided to put a group together for an overnight ghost hunt. I had some professor friends in that department so I joined them."

Does he think the Pen is haunted? John says "Yes! I had an experience while there that night. It was in one of the cell blocks, maybe North Hall, I'm not sure? I was with two professor friends from OU and we were up on the top tier of the cell block. All night long I had been letting a tape recorder record from my shirt pocket. We came down from the top tier, banging our feet on the metal catwalks and stairs, clanging metal doors. At the bottom we opened and closed a metal door that slammed closed with a loud "bang!" When I got home and played back the tape, I heard again our loud footsteps, all the clanging and banging, and our conversations. When we closed that last door, I heard it slam shut on the tape, followed immediately by a man's voice saying in a low tone, "Boom!" It was very clear and I knew it was not my voice nor was it the voice of either of my friends. I played the tape for them later and they were startled and afraid when they heard the voice. They agreed that the voice did not belong to them. We three were the only people in the cell block at that time." Check out John's website www.jkachuba.com

Dawn Chance lives in Alliance, Ohio in Stark County and is an Operations Supervisor for Subway restaurants and felt amazement the first time she saw the Pen. Dawn was on a ghost hunt with Haunted Heartland Tours as a birthday present and thinks the Pen is haunted as had some experiences that night. She felt icy cold air and the feeling of being watched.

Amy from Marietta Ohio is a homemaker with a passion for spirits and ghosts. She and her husband Mike came along with their friend Jeff and explore the Pen on May 29th 2010. She had this to say about their night in the old prison "My husband and our friend had an overnight ghost hunt on May 29, 2010 and it was pretty interesting! We got some great pictures with orbs and a pretty scary looking face in the mirror in the bathroom in the infirmary. When we were in the Hole, we were asking the spirits to give us a sign that they were here and all of a sudden a brick hit the floor right in front of us! While we were in the Sugar Shack we sat in the dark for a while and nothing happened so we decided to go somewhere else. As we were walking out a light bulb exploded right in front of us. We have no idea where it came from... especially since there are no light bulbs down there!!!"

It's amazing how many families get involved in the hobby of ghost hunting. One of these examples is **Beth and Joshua DeVore**. Beth is a government worker. Her son Joshua hangs out with his mom at some of the hunts she attends. Beth lives in North Canton Ohio and has been hunting for about nine years. They came to the Pen for the first time in 2007 and their first thought was, "WOW! It looked like something out of a gothic novel" They both said they had a feeling of heaviness and sadness in some areas. Beth relates the experience that night "I thought it was the Sugar Shack, but Joshua says no. It was the area that has the picnic tables in it. (The Alamo) We were all sitting on the tables listening to the guide tell about the area. I felt a hand grab my upper thigh. I slapped my son, and said "Stop that, it's not funny." He said" Mom what are you talking about?" I didn't move. The lady behind us stated, "He didn't touch you." To this day my son insists it was not his hand that grabbed my leg.

Dianne Blosser is a member of the Boo Crew PI and lives in Canton, Ohio. She is a talented photographer and can often be seen walking in various cemeteries and haunted locations trying to get that "perfect shot." She has been investigating the paranormal for nearly ten years. The first time she laid eyes on the prison her thought was "It's big and creepier then I thought it would be." I would imagine that thought entered many a convicts mind.

In her interview I asked Dianne "What do you think is the most "active" area of the Pen? She says for her it's the "The boiler room and the psych ward." I asked her why and what had happened. Dianne said "Oh geez, we have had so many experiences it seems. The two that stand out most in my mind are the time we were standing outside of Red's cell and feeling a chilly breeze rush in between us and someone asked "Red are you here" and I picked a gravely male voice responding "Yeah" on my recorder."

Dianne continues "Another time we were leaving the psych ward (I guess it was the back entrance) the entrance over the room with all the paintings. We were walking down a narrow hallway kind of single file when the EMF meter I was carrying, started going off then about ten seconds later we heard a loud bang from behind us coming from the area we just left. We stopped turned around but nothing more happened. It was like something ran past us and slammed a door behind us. If something was setting of the EMF meter at that moment...I couldn't find the source. I walked all over that hallway trying to get it to happen again...it was dead!"

Sylvia Triesel comes along on ghost hunts not only for the thrill, but also for the history. She lives in Akron, Ohio and is not a member of an organized group but that doesn't stop her from traveling all over exploring old haunts. The first time she investigated the Pen was in July 2010. She doesn't claim to be psychic or a sensitive but has had a few unusual experiences. Sylvia says that the first time she saw the prison, she was "Awestruck at the size and the architecture." She believes that there is paranormal activity that occurs at the site and for her, the most active areas are the Psych Ward and where the Death House used to stand. (North Yard)

Sylvia had an experience in the Death House area that she shared with us. "Chani and I were investigating the area where the Death House once stood. It is a paved parking area now and recreational area. Our EMF meter started to go off. We started to look for reasons for the meter to be registering. We could not find a reason for this to be happening. We were standing in the middle of an open area. We decided to take a few steps backwards and the meter stopped. We asked that whatever was making the meter register to follow us. The meter started to register again. We took two more steps back and the same thing happened, the meter stopped we again asked to follow us, the meter registered again. We did the same thing for a third time with the exact same results. The fourth time we stepped back, the meter stopped, we waited and no EMF detection. We asked that if it would make the meter go off one more time that we would leave the area. The meter went off once. We kept to our word and left the area. We went back to that same area about an hour later and found no EMF readings. This is the first time that we have had what seems to be responses using an EMF meter. We both think that we were interacting with some type of intelligent energy."

Sylvia relates her Psych Ward experience, "We had two EVPs captured in the psychiatric ward on April 25, 2009. Chani, Matt and I had just passed the x-ray area and entered into a large room. Matt and I heard a knocking sound coming from the corner of the room; we went to investigate and could not determine what the noise was. The three of us were the only ones on the floor at this time. Matt asked, "Is there anyone here with us"? A reply from a male voice was captured on my digital recorder stating "Mike McGee 21." Forty-five seconds later a male voice whispered "Go away". The question remains who was Mike McGee 21, an inmate, guard or a worker? Research of the records may answer these questions.

Sylvia realizes that research is very important when conducting paranormal investigations.

Becky McKinnell is a teacher in Ohio and a volunteer at the Ohio State Reformatory. (www.mrps.org) She loves exploring old historical locations and can be found, on most weekends, leading folks around the Reformatory in Mansfield, Ohio. On one weekend away, she ventured to the Pen with her ghost hunting partner, Jill. Becky has this to say about that night in particular. "Jill and I got a cool EVP up in the Psych Ward. Unfortunately the only thing that I experienced was in the Psych ward. I was back in one of the examination rooms by myself and Jill was in the hallway and it has been the only time in the 11 years that I've been ghost hunting that I felt an overwhelming need to get out of there... just a very uneasy feeling. Not much of a story but the EVP that Jill got was great!"

Edward Talkington hails from Massillon, Ohio. Ed has his own group called Talkington Paranormal Research and has been investigating the paranormal for over ten years. I asked him if he had any psychic abilities and he told me he was "paranormally inept!" He has been to the Pen twice so far. On July 24th in 2010, Ed joined us for an investigation and this is what he had to say; "I was amazed at how clean it was compared to the Mansfield Reformatory. The Adena mound across the street is fascinating." Ed continues on with his views, "I believe there is more to death than what most people realize. I'm a firm believer in Einstein's theory that energy cannot be created or destroyed; it can only be changed from one form to another. I then asked Ed if he thought the Pen was haunted and if he had any experiences he wanted to share. "I personally have no hard data to confirm or deny but I would venture to say the Sugar Shack or Boiler Room is the most active area. I didn't have an experience that night but a team member (Jennifer

Longfellow) who is sensitive, felt heavy pressure on her hands (like her hands were being squeezed) while walking through the courtyard on the July 24th trip last month with Haunted Heartland."

Everyone has preferences when it comes to gear they carry and Ed is no different. He says, "I personally enjoy watching through an IR camera but I really couldn't choose one device over the other."

Peggy Batista is a person who you meet and instantly like. Bubbly, smart and pretty, it's easy to see why she can light up a room when she walks into it. It's also a great reason to hang out with her in a prison full of 'manly' spirits. It's been my experience that whatever attracted you in life, will attract you in the great beyond. Just as personality traits exist (stubbornness, mischievous, grumpy etc...) among the living, it also can continue in the 'aura' of an entity. So bring a female into a prison where men lived, and see what can happen!

Peggy lives in Uniontown, Ohio, and is a 40 something Teacher and Paralegal. She has been investigating the paranormal for over 10 years and first came to the Pen in 2009. Peggy says she is sensitive and can feel and see ghosts/spirits and can occasionally hear them. When she saw the Pen for the first time, her initial impression was, "Wow, it's so close to the road!"

Peg came along that night because a friend asked me to come to a private hunt to celebrate her birthday. The Sugar Shack is where she thinks the most activity was at that night. What happened at that time? Peg said "In the dark it felt as if someone was "invading" my space and then someone took a picture and the flash went off and there was a man standing right next to me, I was a little surprised how well I could see him for a split second and then as I started to walk away something tugged at my hair. Very cool!"

Cheyrl Kneram is a volunteer and tour guide at the Ohio State Reformatory. Cheyrl lives in Cuyahoga Falls, and is a housewife when she is not off investigating the paranormal! She is a Mansfield Reformatory Ghost Hunt Volunteer, and has been there for ten years in that capacity. (www.mrps.org)

She first investigated the Pen at a 2007 Public hunt and again in 2009 at a private hunt. I asked her if she was psychic, a medium or sensitive to paranormal activity. Her response, "I think everyone has some ability if they know how to or want to use it." She was interested in the building and its claim of paranormal activity which is what drew her to investigate. Cheyrl has a very practical opinion of the paranormal. She says "Yes, I believe in the paranormal but still stay a skeptic because not everything is paranormal. Debunk!"

I asked Cheyrl if she thought the Pen were haunted and if she had any experiences while investigating that she cared to share. "Yes it has to be haunted after all the pain it's held in those walls. There has to be residual energy there from the tragedies that occurred while it was open. The most active area for me was where R.D. was slain, the Boiler room. One problem is fighting the Bats down there long enough to investigate! I think the Boiler room, Visitation area, Psych Ward, and the Gym are the most active."

Cheyrl told us what happened that night, "In the Boiler room I captured an EVP of a man saying "over here." In the Visitation Area I heard whispering coming from the hall where the famous Shadow Man photo was taken. We then heard what sounded like pebbles being thrown at us in the room. In the Psych Ward during a private hunt around 4:00 a.m. and I was going up by myself to get the last four people left in the building. During my walk up there I was hearing a woman talking ahead of me however there was no one there. In the old Gym room the floor was very bad. The people in the tour group were taking turns stepping in and out of the room to get to see it. When I stepped into that room I saw a shadow man in the corner... however once again there was no one there. During the day tour while I was by Red Snyder's Cell I got touched twice on my shoulder and then another friend beside me was touched also." I asked her Cheyrl what her favorite equipment was to use. She replied "Tape recorders or videos cameras are needed to document with, however a lot of the tools I find distract me and I was always missing the cool stuff!"

Karyn Gaugler is from Wadsworth, Ohio and is a Medical Receptionist and Paranormal Investigator. She tells us about her first investigation at the Pen. "It was my first trip to the Pen, and I went with my friend and fellow investigator Mary. We were told the story about the riot that had happened where three men were beaten, stabbed and thrown down a set of steps to die. Those steps have since been filled in, but were still a source of paranormal activity. We decided to do an EVP session where the steps used to be, and as we were getting ready to start, I heard in my right ear a man moaning in pain. I turned my flashlight in both directions, but no man....nobody there. It was as if I was hearing those same men still moaning in pain. That was the best experience I have ever had in investigating, and it happened at the WV Pen!"

Curt Talley hails from West Virginia and has been to the Pen many times. He claims to have been scratched on the back by something or someone he could not see, but cannot wait to go back again.

Brian Cook from Hilliard, Ohio is an IT Engineer and Paranormal Investigator. His experience was a bit frightening. "I was with another paranormal investigator were in Red's cell. We were using a Frank's Box. Soon as we turned it on, it started saying "Leave Now, Leave, Go, Go, Die, Kill." It was very freaky especially since he was killed in front of his cell and he was notorious at that prison. We went in June of 2009."

Carol Breckenfeld is a fifty-something investigator who loves the adventure of a good hunt. She lives in Lake Geneva, WI and is in Law Enforcement. She is the founder of GSI (Ghost Scene Investigations) and is the Lead Investigator. The group purposefully does not have a website. Carol says, "This puts our "clients" to ease that nothing from their house or place of business will be posted. All evidence we gather belongs to the client to do what they will with it." Carol has been walking into the shadows of the night with gear in hand for fifteen plus years. She has been to the Pen on only one occasion saw far. She shares her thoughts on investigating and the hunt at the Pen for us. "We were to Moundsville in April of 2010 for a night time ghost hunt. Over the years I have developed a sense that helps me investigate. I thought, "Hot damn…this is gonna be fun!" when I saw the Pen for the first time. My daughter is a cop and she came along."

Carol sheds some light on her ghost hunt experience. "I will tell you of the incident in the Sugar Shack. It was just myself, my daughter, Rita and a lady who came for her first ghost hunt by herself. Rita had situated herself by one of the pillars, and was videotaping towards me to capture an EVP session we were going to have. Whilst in the middle of this session, Rita felt a cold spot near her. With my Mel meter we were able to document a twelve degree cold spot. This spot moved across Rita to her elbow. During this time we captured many EVP's. Apparently the ghosts talk amongst themselves...we got "I see a cop" (Rita is a police officer) "She's a cop!" and various other evp's. Right when the cold spot settled by Rita's elbow, her arm was pushed by something unseen. Immediately after this there was cracking wood sound coming from the area behind the pillar Rita was sitting in front of. The lady that was with us used her thermometer along with the Mel meter to document a 12 degree temperature change with the cold spot. Within two minutes, the cold spot had dissipated and there was no more cold spot."

Carol offers up other experiences on that active night. "Here are three more experiences we had at Moundsville that night. First one is the first room to the right on the Psych floor. Rita and I were in there alone on the entire floor, doing what we do....filming our evp session. We heard loud footsteps coming up the stairs onto the landing, and into the hallway right up to the door of the room we were in. Rita expressed her opinion that I should note the disturbance as humans. I said to her...maybe not! I immediately went out to the hall...nobody was there....I went to the stairwell and landing...nobody there! I tried to recreate the heaviness of the footsteps we heard...I could not stomp loud enough to recreate it. Rita was dumbfounded!"

"Second and third experiences were on the fourth tier of the West, at least that's where I think we were. I was standing behind as Rita went down the tier calling out the inmates as a Police Officer would. As she got down the tier, I saw a dark waist high shape come out of a cell in front of her. I said, "Rita, there is something moving in front of you".....Rita replied, "I see it!" At this point the thing charged right at Rita...backing her up on the tier, and moved through her. As it passed me I felt an icy cold that I know from many years of ghost hunting to be the real deal. It took a few minutes before we could continue."

Carol continues "Later that night we told the lady who experienced our Sugar Shack cold spots with us about our experience on the fourth tier. She was eager to go see where this took place. We went back. Again, we were the only ones at the location. We were walking down the tier. Rita first, then me, then our lady friend. As Rita and I passed the cell that the thing had first come out of....the lady was following up the end. As she passed in front of the cell...she was spit on!! It was not a drop of water coming from the ceiling as it came sideways out of the cell. She had it on the side of her face and we checked it...it was spit, not water! It was quite an experience for all of us."

Ron White and Jane Mayfield are made for each other! The first night I met them was the very night they were married. It was in front of the Pen administration building. They ghost hunted with us on their honeymoon and then headed off the next day for a haunted New England tour with a night at the Lizzie Borden house. Can you even imagine?

Ron and Jane live in Morgantown, West Virginia and started a group called Haunted Spectre (www.hauntedspectre.com) and have been investigating the paranormal for nearly years. They have journeyed to the Pen every single year since 2005. Ron says, "We started out with just the day tours. After a couple years, we decided to try the night ghost hunts and fell in love with the prison and the idea of ghost hunting. We have been on many night time hunts and recently had our own group there on our own. We are somewhat sensitive to sensations and the feeling of being watched or followed. I've seen shadows, and heard voices when nobody is around. Just played it off as just my imagination, but now, I'm not so sure. The first time we saw the building we thought it was awesome and beautiful. The "gothic" motif and just the massiveness of the entire building was mesmerizing. It literally took our breath away! We both had an interest in the paranormal and while online one night, we looked for haunted places in WV and found a link for the prison. We decided to go check it out and are very glad we did. It has become our home away from home. We believe in the paranormal even more so now than we did before we started doing investigations. Although we haven't personally had the experiences that many others have had, we certainly do believe that the prison is haunted.

I asked Ron and Jane what the most "active" area of the Pen was for them. Ron replied, "For us, it would have to be the Wagon Gate. That is where we have had our experiences at. We have had other experiences in other areas, but none like we had in the wagon gate. Other locations would be The Hole, and Solitary Confinement.

I asked them about their experiences and this is what they shared with me, "In the Wagon Gate, we both experienced a heaviness that made it difficult to breathe and our legs ached like we were carrying a heavy weight around the place." Jane offered. She continued with, "Even after leaving the Wagon Gate, the heaviness stayed with us for awhile. In Solitary Confinement, Ron became cold, right down to the bone. Even with a coat on, the cold was almost unbearable. It started the moment he walked into the area and lasted until we walked out to the recreation area." Ron says, "In the Hole, Jane has had her hair stroked." We wish Ron and Jane many years of haunted, happy bliss.

Anmarie Gumm of Clinton, Ohio is a Registered Nurse who likes to investigate the paranormal. This is her experience from her very first visit, "My husband and I were in the Boiler room during two experiences. The first was while we were recording in an attempt to catch any EVP's and we asked for any proof that there was someone there with us. We at that point were able to hear and catch (on our recorder) what sounded like something being thrown. We later moved to another location in the Boiler room and were able to catch an amazing EVP. We were sitting in two of the three chairs and I had laid my recorder on the 3rd chair. We then were asking for a chair to be moved or any noise. At that point I had an overwhelming sense of "something" rushing at me? In response, I said, "Oh f***" and on the recorder you immediately hear, "f***"! We did not hear it during, but realized it later while listening to our recordings. I wish I could explain what I felt. It was like someone rushing at you and I actually tensed up pulling both of my shoulders up, expecting to be knocked right off my chair! I went in as an "optimistic pessimist" and left a believer!

I cannot wait to return. My husband also was not able to enter the one part of the boiler room without the hair on his arms standing straight up; which we did photograph. We did also capture a picture of an orb. I took the pictures back to back in a dark room that got my attention somehow. You can see the orb, on the floor in the first picture, and merely an outline of it in the next picture taken seconds later. If it is enlarged it has a greenish glow to it, unlike any I have seen before. Definitely an awesome experience! We cannot wait to do more with Sherri Brake due to her experience and her amazing professionalism. Thanks, West Virginia!"

Kristie Kirsch Kristi lives in Chapmanville, West Virginia but lived in Ohio when she first visited the Pen. She was the Founder and Case Manager of the group based out of Canton, Ohio and has been investigating for many years but has not been active in the past few years. The Now Life sometimes gets in the way of the After Life. Kristie says,

"Ever since, I can remember I have always been interested in the paranormal. I have always enjoyed a good ghost story and history. Occasionally, she has been called to do independent cases but would love to be more active again.

So far Kristie has been to the Pen on two occasions for overnight hunts Saturday, March 20, 2010 and Saturday, July 24, 2010. Both times she was with Haunted Heartland Tours. She claims not to be sensitive or psychic but has this opinion on it, "I have always heard that everyone has a psychic ability, it is like a muscle and that the more that you use it or react to it the stronger it will become. I have found that the more investigations that I go on I have found that I am becoming more sensitive, I am able to now hear low rumbling, as if conversations are taking place."

I asked Kristie what her first impression upon seeing the Pen for the first time. She replied, "My initial impression upon seeing the pen for the first time was that of awe. The architecture of the Pen is reminiscent of some of the greatest fortresses of Europe. To stand in front of it, you marvel at its size. In your mind's eye, you are immediately drawn back in time, thinking of the prisoners that may have stood in the same spot, knowing that they too saw the exact same image. Most knowing, that they would never see the outside of these walls again."

When asked if she believes in the paranormal, Kristie said "That is still to be determined. I know that there are a lot of unexplained things in this world, things I cannot explain and do not have answers for. As far as thinking that the site is haunted? I think that the Pen has more than its share of unexplained things."

I asked Kristie about any activity she may have encountered and if so, what and where. She said, "There are a couple active spots that we have found in our investigations of the pen. One is the Sugar Shack and the other is the Maximum Security cell with the Rolling Stone's bid red mouth painted on the wall. (Author's note, Danny Lehman's cell #2 A side in North Hall) Kristie added "The Sugar Shack was where I had an experience. On March 20, 2010, my friend, a guy, and I were investigating the Sugar Shack. The time was approximately 2:30 a.m. and all the lights were out, of course. My friend, Beth and I were sitting on a bench that was against the wall. The bench was no more than an inch from the wall to its back. Beth was sitting to my right, and there was space in between us, as both of us were making use of the armrests. The guy that was with us was standing approximately six to eight feet away to my left. I had my KII meter, on my right knee. We had found a plastic dragon toy and placed it on the floor in front of us. Beth was asking questions, trying to get someone to communicate, to move the dragon, or make the KII meters light up. Then she said it. Oh, what she said, I will never forget. Beth said, "If you are able to touch us then please do." No more than 30 seconds after those words left her mouth, at the exact same moment, both of us were touched, my hair was petted on the right side and Beth was touched on the left elbow. We both jumped up and I screamed. We immediately then sat back down and asked that we be touched again. We sat for a few minutes longer and nothing else occurred."

Kristie recalls another experience that same night, My friend Beth, a guy that was with us, and myself were investigating the Maximum Security cell block, First floor, the one with the painted Rolling Stones Mouth, I am not sure of the cell number, but it is the first one on the one side. We did an EVP session there, I had mentioned that there were women in his cell and how did he feel about that. Upon playing back the recording we got a voice saying "Women." Also, there was an instance in the North Hall Cell Block on the first floor we were kind of lost. I asked Beth, where is the door. An EVP was captured of a man saying, "They can't find the door".

Kristie continues with more comments about another night of investigating the prison. She said "On July 24, 2010, with a different group of people. We decided to use the KII meter and set up the "Ghostbox" and do a real time EVP session. There were at least 10 people gathered around to watch. We then decided to use playing cards that were bought from the Mansfield Reformatory we would play Blackjack or 21.We first asked if anyone was there. We received confirmation of someone was with us and his name was Joe. We asked if Joe wanted to play cards with us. We received a response of yes. We played several hands, we never looked at the cards, and using the "Ghostbox" with Joe. We asked him to tell us to hit or stand. Joe never busted!"

John Ackerman lives in Alliance Ohio and has been ghost hunting for a few years, believes in the paranormal and thinks the Pen is haunted 'big time". He has ventured to the Pen on seven separate occasions and all were overnight investigations with Haunted Heartland Tours. John came along the first time because a friend asked if he wanted to go on a ghost hunt. He's hooked now!

I asked John if he had experienced anything unusual while at the prison and where it had been if he had. John said "As far as getting EVP's, I have to say it's the gym that is the most active. I have gotten three good EVPS in the Gym, three in the Psych Ward and one in the Boiler room. I also got my right pant pocket tugged on when I was in the boiler room." John's favorite gear to implement on investigations is his digital voice recorder.

Missy Tayse lives in Massillon, Ohio and is a Certified Medical Assistant. She was at the prison on July 24, 2010 and did not get much in the way of physical evidence, but she did have some personal experiences. She captured a few pictures with orbs and used a cassette tape recorder out in the yard where the Sugar Shack is located. She tells us about it, "I walked to a tower at the end of the yard. I captured a voice on the recorder but not sure if it said "Hi" or "Hide." I had two personal experiences, and the first one was in the infirmary and psych area. I didn't like this area. I held on to my husband with my eyes closed while trying to take pictures!

"I felt like people where watching us, popping their heads out of doors and when we got to the steps to go down, it felt like people watching us go down the steps from over the railing. My second experience was in the hallway where the shadow figure has been seen. Someone in front of us had just flashed a picture in the other room and when the light from the flash illuminated the area, there he was in the same spot as in the picture that was in the gift shop. It startled me to the point that I screamed. It was a complete solid black shape."

Brian Fain is the founder of the Massillon Ghost Hunters Society in Massillon, Ohio. Brian founded the group along with his wife, Lena. Brian is also the Case Researcher and a Field Investigator. This is what he says about his interest in the paranormal, "I have always been interested in the paranormal, ever since I was a child and the fascination has never stopped. The thought that the mortal body is no more than a shell, it may age, wither and die but the person who you are shall endure forever in spirit." Brian's favorite spirited quote is "Once you have eliminated all other possibilities; whatever remains, regardless of how improbable it may seem, must be the truth". Brian, along with his group, has visited the Pen and enjoyed the activity it has to offer. The Massillon Ghost Hunters Society came along on the July 19th 2008 expedition with Haunted Heartland Tours. They investigated throughout the entire Pen that evening and focused a great deal of time and energy into debunking a television shows claim. The claim stated that a certain shadow person photograph by Polly Gear, was not paranormal, but was her own shadow instead. Massillon Ghost Hunter Society members that night included Brain, Lena, Carolyn, Christine, Ron, Rick, Sarah, Garann, and Elizabeth.

Donna Callaway lives in Chattaroy, West Virginia where she is a student. Donna is a Paranormal Investigator and Co-founder of the Tri-State GhostHunters. Donna tells us of her experience at the Pen. "I've got an EVP from Red Snyder's cell and it sounds like "get out, leave, drop it". It actually occurred the night of one Sherri Brake's Ghost Hunting 101 classes. On another occasion, my group and I had a lot of responses with our K2 and Ghost Meters. I've got a picture (sequence of 4) of what I believe was following us around. Looks like a man, with glasses and a hat, taken in solitary. I've submitted three of the pictures in their evidence contest." Donna says she has been at the prison more times than she can count. Now that's a dedicated researcher!

Tim and Laura Oppihle are a husband and wife who share the hobby of ghost hunting. They live in Akron, Ohio and have been to the Pen once so far. They recall their night time ghost hunt on June 19, 2009. "While investigating in the yard by the chapel, we saw a shadow come out of a door on the far end of the wall. As my wife and I were walking toward the wall the shadow, it darted to our left of the exercise equipment. We shined our flashlights at the spot where we saw the shadow go and no one was there. As we go closer to the wall, the shadow darted back to where we first saw it appear. We chased the shadow for about 15-20 minutes before we got tired of trying to catch it. Finally we walked up to where we first saw the shadow emerge from the door, only to find that there was no door there. It was a truly unique experience as we both felt that the shadow was playing games with us."

Laura Oppihle is married to Tim who volunteered his experience in the above paragraph. Laura was quick to offer her experience as well. "I have some psychic abilities and I investigate with Sherri Brake. I had an EVP of a conversation or broadcast out in the yard at the top of the stairs leading to the Sugar Shack. I was told later that it was the area where the inmates had a radio station. I was asking questions about what the inmates had seen and what brought them into the Pen. I received old time music and static like a radio broadcast. I saw shadows up in the one tower when all this was going on. The whole feel of the area I was in had changed. It seemed cooler and "charged" somehow and very sad. I got overwhelmed with sadness and had to leave. All in all it was an eye opening experience. I can't wait to visit again. I hope the spirits remember me!"

Sharon O'Dell is a 36 year old office manager living in Summersville, West Virginia. She worked at the West Virginia Pen from 1994-1995 in the capacity of Shift Commander for Dayshift. Sharon is a bit sensitive to the paranormal and can see and feel entities. She was very impressed with the size of the Pen when approaching it for the first time. I asked Sharon if she experienced anything unexplainable while working there. This is what she told me, "I experienced many unusual sightings and sounds. There are windows in my office that lead out into the 'main hall'. It was very common on evening and night shift to see someone quickly walk past the window. This would happen during times when we were on lockdown and <u>no</u> inmates were allowed out of their cells. No officers were in the hall, and with the length of the hall, no one could get out of the hall faster than you could get from the desk to the window. I never found anyone in the hall when this occurred. It became so common that I stopped looking down the hall, just laughed it off as ghosts."

I asked Sharon about the inmates and what she encountered from the living. "I remember many of them. Some of the inmates that were considered 'the worst of the worst' happened to be the ones that gave me the least amount of trouble." Sharon told me, "I have found it to be situational with certain people and certain times. They are inmates, they will not respond to yelling or bullying. They will also respond to a uniform. Especially ones that would be deemed "Long Timers".

I was curious if she ever noticed a pattern to the activity and where the hot spots were in her opinion. She says she noticed most activity happening on evening and night shift. I asked where the most active locations seemed to have been. She said, "Anywhere in the basement and also in the Old Admin part of the building. A few in P&R. and very few in SPU unit, due to it holding inmates at the time." Sharon said, "I have had the feeling at times of being completely surrounded when I was in a room all alone. I have had my hair touched and the sleeves of my uniform tugged on." Sharon is not the only one who has had that happen to her. Many ladies have had unusual and unexplainable occurrences while working at the Pen in the past, or investigating it after its closing in 1995.

Cortney Fish from Ohio works as a Human Resource Rep. She visited the West Virginia Penitentiary with her boyfriend and had a great time. When asked if anything paranormal happened she said that her boyfriend was touched in the Sugar Shack...and it was not by her.

Brian Cook from Hilliard, Ohio is an Engineer and a Paranormal Investigator. He said that he and another friend were in Red Snyder's cell in North Hall and they were using a Franks Box. (For Electronic Voice Phenomena) Brian said that as soon as they turned it on, it began to say, "Leave now, leave, go, go, die, kill". Brian said "It was freaky especially since we knew Red was killed right where we were standing. This was in June of 2009." I'm not sure how long Brian and his buddy hung around after that. Most people would've left quickly, I'm sure!

Debbie Green has been on quite a few ghost hunts with Haunted Heartland Tours. You could say she is a familiar face! Deborah hails from Akron, Ohio and considers herself a sensitive with being able to see and hear spirit. She is part of ghost hunting group called WASH (We are Still Here) and is the lead investigator and founder. She was 12 years old when she did her first investigation of the paranormal so she has been at it for awhile. Debbie says, "My first visit to the West Virginia Pen was a birthday gift from my two sons. I have been hooked ever since then! I am a believer in the paranormal and I think the most active areas of the Pen would be the Wagon Gate and the Psych Ward. I get plenty of EVPs in the Psych Ward! One time while I was in the Psych Ward, I saw a shadow run from the room into the hallway. It also went into the room with the dental equipment. I asked while in this area "How many pissed off inmates are in here?" and received the number "72" while listening to my EVP session later."

Debbie continues on "On March 28, 2009, I conducted an EVP session in Solitary. I asked "What did you do in here while sitting here 23 hours a day?" I got replies. "Nothing" and "I was bored." In the Sugar Shack area I asked if anybody wanted to talk to me and the table where I had my bottle of water, KII, and recorder shook hard and my water splashed in the bottle. I have been to the WV Pen three times. March 28, 2009, April 20, 2009 and March 20 2010. I love that place! I averaged about 12-15 EVP's each time I went."

Debbie Weaver investigated the building in the summer of 2011. This is her description of her evening of family fun, "My sister, Laura Templin, my husband Tom, and I came to WV Penitentiary on Friday September 9 of 2011. I am 55, Tom is 56, and Laura is 50 years old and we were extremely excited to be coming on this ghost hunt! My sister and I are a little bit sensitive. I don't know if this is due to the fact we have been living with spirits in our houses for the last five years and are just in tune with them, or pay attention more than most people. We drove to West Virginia from Cleveland, Ohio. When we first got there, the prison looked formidable, dark, and spooky! We brought some equipment we have bought over the years. A K-2 meter, a Mel meter, a night vision camcorder, laser grid, 2 digital cameras, and 5 audio recorders and a bunch of flashlights and batteries. We started investigating around 1AM in the courtyard by the chapel. We got some hits on the K-2, but not much else. We went into the Sugar Shack, and again, got nothing. We tried the boiler room, the Wagon Gate, the courtyard outside of it, the place where the older prisoners were held, and maximum security. We were getting hits on the K-2 and the Mel, but nothing much else. It was almost time to leave, and we decided to head to the cafeteria, we had not been there yet. Not much was going on there either. Laura and I decided to wander into the kitchen area. (Tom had sat down in the cafeteria, and did not feel like getting up. His loss!) As soon as we walked in, both of us felt sick to our stomachs, and the room felt heavy and oppressive. We both knew 'something' or 'someone' was there. Right away we started getting hits with the K-2, (all the way to red many times), and the Mel meter was reading up to 8.2 at one time. I saw a shadow run from right to left, very fast. We started an EVP session and were asking questions when we received a response when we asked for a name. We did not know we got a response at that time, but next time I come to the WV Pen, the first place I am heading is the kitchen so I can find Carlos! After about 10 minutes of EVP work, we both started feeling really nauseous, and it was really getting creepy. We started to hear noises all around us, and had the feeling we were being surrounded. (Sounds paranoid, but that is what we felt.) I told Laura I had to leave, I really was sick, and we started to leave, and we heard someone behind us, and we actually RAN out of the kitchen! It was the most awesome and intense experience we have had in a long, long time. And we had just discussed when we were in the cafeteria, about how none of us had been frightened, or even felt creeped out, and then Carlos came along. We can NOT wait till next year, so we can come again. It was a pleasure meeting you Sherri, and I want to thank you for your hospitality. We had a great time, and yes, we believe the prison is haunted. Rather, we KNOW the prison is haunted!! We did catch other EVPS, a lot of which we can't make out what is being said. One sounds like 'help me', another sounds like someone is screaming. Thanks again for the visit and we had a chillingly great time!!"

Connie McMasters is no stranger to the paranormal. She has been investigating for over 30 years and is a spry 60 something who hails from New York State. Connie has ventured to every big haunted location we have featured in our tours and never hesitates to head into the dark. She counts the WV Pen has one of the most haunted locations she has ever been too and says there are so many numerous paranormal experiences she has had, that she has lost track. Connie's mother was a psychic and had worked at Lilly Dale back in the 1970's so she comes by it naturally. She is one to shun the use of equipment and prefers to explore and document alone.

Mark Brown is a part-time member of Ohio P.A.S.T. Paranormal and Spirit Trackers. He is in his mid 40's and lives in Florence, Ky. He is employed as a security officer but loves to find time to investigate. I asked him what equipment he likes to use and what his experiences have been. "I mainly use my video camera, and my flashlight with a green lens, although I carry other equipment like a Frank Ghost Box and an EMF detector. I go to investigate for two reasons: to obtain evidence and to help lost souls cross over to the spirit world. I have helped four other souls cross over at Trans Allegheny Lunatic Asylum, although I do not claim to be an expert. Anyway, I first went to the Psych ward and heard loud banging like it was coming from inside the cells. I did not take time to debunk this. I do not know about the pipes in the building, or anything like that, but it did sound like someone was inside the cells."

"Anyway, when I went to the Sugar Shack there was a group having a flashlight session and the woman asked if the spirit needed help and it said 'yes'. I asked her permission to ask questions and she said go ahead. I asked if the person wanted to cross over all they had to do it to ask Heavenly Father to take you home, and to not be afraid. I then felt a rush inside my chest when this happened. This happens when you cross someone over. The woman then asked if other spirits were down there and according to the answers from the flashlight it was affirmative. This was on Sept 10th, 2011 with Haunted Heartland Tours. I haven't looked at my videos yet, but I do have a picture of a shadow person taken by my digital camera. I enjoy finding evidence, but I also feel good about helping a lost soul crossing over to the spirit world."

Mason Recco has been to the prison on multiple overnighters since he was 16 years old. He has had so many experiences that he hopes to write a book one day on the subject. His favorite locations in the Pen include the Boiler room and the Psych Ward. He is the son of the author.

Dani Weathers came along with us at Haunted Heartland Tours for an overnight hunt on Sept 9-10 of 2011. She says she is a "newbie" at investigating, and that she may be a bit sensitive to the paranormal.

I asked her a series of questions. What was your first impression of the WV Pen? Dani said "SCARY. I got some creepy vibes and I felt a lot of sadness that emanated from the empty darkness of a lot of the rooms." I then asked her if she brought along any gear to help her investigate. She said, "As a beginner, I didn't have anything super fancy. Just a cheap Ben and Howell night vision camcorder and a digital recorder. And a flashlight (most important thing ha-ha)!" Oh Dani, if you only knew how many people showed up at dark haunts with NO flashlights! Anyway, Dani hails from Columbus, Ohio where she is a shift manager at TanPro USA. She, just like a few other "lucky" people in the Pen, had an unusual experience. Dani tells us "In the sugar shack we walked in on another group having an intense experience with a ghost, and we sat down to watch. It was so incredible! They would ask 'yes' or 'no' questions and for every 'yes', the ghost would turn on a flashlight. Now, this flashlight had a top that you twist to turn on, not something that would easily turn on just by itself. It was crazy. But then, when one of their group started walking around with an EMF meter, it went off around me and they asked the ghost if he was sitting near me, and the flashlight turned on, meaning yes! Yes, this ghost took a liking to me. We never figured out why, but he said it was because I reminded him of someone (from a yes or no question we had asked). After a few minutes, I started to feel dizzy and nauseous – it was hard just to formulate a single thought, let alone try and tell someone I wasn't feeling well. I turned to a guy who I was sitting by and tried to tell him that something was wrong with me, that I could barely keep my head up. I was so scared, and I wanted to cry. Luckily the guy knew exactly what was happening – the ghost was drawing on my energy and he immediately told me to concentrate on something, anything, to keep me focused (which was a lot easier said than done, I might add). It was an incredible feeling. You hear about this kind of experience on TV shows, like on Ghost Adventures whenever Nick says that he's feeling all the same symptoms I had. It was something else to actually experience it! My boyfriend was absolutely terrified for me though! But I welcomed the ghost drawing on my energy if it meant he would be able to stick around a little longer and answer more of our questions (I even told the ghost he was welcome to use my energy if it helped him). I left the Sugar Shack freezing and shivering, despite the humid heat outside and in the building itself. My boyfriend had to give me his sweater (and I was already wearing one) for several minutes so the goose bumps would go away and my teeth would stop chattering!

She continues, "For my first ghost hunt, I never imagined something like that would happen to me! It still gives me goose bumps when I share what happened to me with others. But I'd do it all over again!"

I asked Dani, "What was your favorite area to check out, and do you think the Pen is paranormally active and if so, did you have an experience?" She replied, "The Sugar Shack is active! Something was definitely in the Boiler room, but we didn't have anything crazy. And the medical ward gave me the absolute CREEPS. Something was there that was oppressive and didn't like us, I felt. I hated being in that area, which just made being there all the more of an experience!"

For a twenty-year old who had never been ghost hunting before, Dani seemed to have a good grip on the nights paranormal activity. From my many overnight visits to the Pen, we have had a handful of people who have refused to go past the lobby. They think they are ready for an overnight experience and then once they see the building and venture inside, they don't want to go any further. They sat in the lobby all night and no amount of persuasion can get them up off their seats and down a darkened hallway. I asked Dani my next question. Do you think the Pen is haunted?? "YES. YES. YES. Any non-believers would 100% believe after one trip there." Yep, I thought. She's hooked!

Dani also had other comments, too. She said, "I liked other things that night. The camaraderie and everyone was helpful. My boyfriend and I actually teamed up with a father and his daughter, people we had just randomly met in the Boiler room when our investigations first started, and the people who had been in the Sugar Shack were so nice. They even left their flashlight for me since the ghost liked me and they were ready to move on. It was cool to be around so many people who shared your passion and beliefs. Though, I wish I had gotten the memo on the all black attire, ha-ha. I felt a little silly in my bright blue sweater. And of course, I loved my experience in the Sugar Shack! Since I've told my friends about what happened to me, some many people want to try out ghost hunting and seeing if they too will experience something beyond the realm of the living."

North Coast Paranormal Investigations is a small group based in Ohio. Though newly formed, their members have been doing paranormal investigations for several years. On

September 3, 2010, a N.C.P.I. team of 20 investigators visited the prison overnight. The team encountered paranormal activity in virtually every area of the prison that was investigated. They gathered photographic evidence throughout, EVPS's in the infirmary and psych ward, and EMF readings and temperature changes in several areas. Team members also experienced audible noises, some upon request, whispering and laughing. One team member was fortunate enough to experience physical sensation while walking through one of the hallways, when he felt a cold presence seemingly move through him. Another, while in the "hole" felt a presence and heard sound beside her, while at the same time high EMF readings were recorded around her. After investigating Moundsville, we believe there is convincing evidence of paranormal activity. You can visit their website at www.northcoastparanorm.com. Their evidence has also been seen on A&E Biography's My Ghost Story.

Investigators of the Past are a paranormal research society located in Northeast Ohio. Their mission is to assist individuals who believe they are experiencing a haunting, paranormal activity, or other unexplained phenomena. Kyle Doneyko is the Founder/Investigator of Investigators of the Past (ITP). He attended a paranormal conference in early 2008 and launched ITP soon after. His main responsibility is to ensure all aspects of the society function effectively. He likes to assist in all areas of the organization to meet new people and gain new experiences. While on investigations, Kyle approaches everything with a purely skeptical outlook. If it can possibly be something normal, then it probably is. Kyle says if they can't disprove the evidence, then they classify it as paranormal.

Trina O'Dell is the Case Manager and Investigator for ITP. As the case manager, she is responsible for handling the incoming requests for investigations, conducting a preliminary interview with clients, and providing the team with the necessary information and background to conduct the investigation.

Lori Robinson is an Investigator with the group and is a school bus driver. She became interested in the paranormal world after watching a couple episodes of Ghost Hunters. She cannot recall ever having any paranormal experiences in her lifetime, except for one incident after her grandmother had passed. It could have been a dream she says, but she thought she had heard her grandmother say to her that "everything will be okay."

Gail Scott is also an Investigator for ITP. She states her passion for this field of work comes from not only the experiences she has had with paranormal activity, but also because of her beliefs. She truly believes there is another realm of existence after the spirit leaves the body. Working as an investigator with ITP allows her to further explore her beliefs, gain a better understanding of the spiritual world, and provide assistance to those experiencing a ghostly encounter or paranormal activity.

The Moundsville Penitentiary Investigation was an incredible experience for ITP. However, they say they believe this gothic fortress holds more than what it revealed to them during the night of their investigation. They say they definitely think this is a place that is active and that they need to return. You can check out their website at: www.investigatorsofthepast.com

CHAPTER 6
SHADOW MAN SIGHTINGS

As most investigators know, Shadow People are elusive. The majority of the time that you come across these fleeting entities, they disappear as quickly as they appeared. Many theories abound in regards to these shadows and the jury- for the most part- is still out. Some claim they are negative entities, others believe them to me harbingers of doom. Nevertheless, it can be startling when you come across one of them.

What exactly is a Shadow Man or person? Shadow people are a very common phenomena in the paranormal field. Known to be quite elusive, these shadowy beings often appear out of the corner of your eye only to vanish when your attention is drawn to them. This elusiveness leads many to wonder if there is intelligence behind their visits. Shadow people can vary in form, but most commonly are said to take the shape of a tall man.

Multiple sightings of Shadow People have occurred repeatedly at the prison. One of the tour guides shares with us her thoughts. "I've seen a shadow man or some kind of human form and I've been talked to by an inmate who was murdered at the prison." **Maggie Gray**, Retired Correctional Officer and current WV Pen Tour Guide.

Tim "Tiny" Myers had his own run in with a shadowy entity and it rocked him to his core. "I never ever thought I would see ANYTHING like that. It caught me and my wife by surprise. It was November and it was so very cold we could see our breath. We were in the Boiler room downstairs and we were all alone after a big group had just left the area. I turned to Karen and shined my flashlight at her over in the corner. She walked away from the corner but standing there behind her a solid figure stood. I freaked out. We left and did not go back." Tim is now a paranormal researcher in western North Carolina and cannot wait to visit the site of his first encounter again.

Kay Ann Simon came on her first ghost hunt at the Pen in 2008. She rode the Haunted Heartland Tour bus from Canton, Ohio to Moundsville, West Virginia and looked forward to having fun. She didn't entertain the possibility of anything paranormal occurring. Skeptic? She hesitated when I asked that.

During her interview she told me "I'm more of a realist and I think more rational then most people, I guess. I don't really believe in this stuff but what I saw early on that morning changed me. It was about 4 am and a few of us were in the Medical area upstairs. I had been looking out one of the dirty windows thinking what a hell this must have been and that's when I felt something on my shoulder. I turned around expecting to see one of my friends there. There was not one around me and that is when I saw movement along the one wall. I stood there and watched as a shadow looking thing stood up. It looked as if it was hunched over and then it just stood up. It walked about two steps and was gone.

I don't think I ever really want to do something (ghost hunt) like this again. Thanks, but no thanks."

I was walking past the entrance into the South Hall area when I saw something run past the cells. I ran into the area and looked shining my flashlight over at where I thought they went. It was a solid wall. I got goose bumps and turned around and walked very quickly back to the lobby. --**Karen from Philadelphia**

Dave Goldinger is a paranormal investigator who lives in NE Ohio and said this about his experience "In the exercise yard I heard voices, saw mists, and felt an overall sense of uneasiness. I did capture a "Shadow Person" inside near the kitchen."

An overnight ghost hunter had this to say about her experience; "Someone in front of us had just flashed a picture in the other room and when the light from the flash illuminated the area, there he was in the same spot as in the picture in the gift shop. It startled me to the point that I screamed. It was a complete solid black shape." **Missy Tayse** shared her story with us a few years ago.

A volunteer from the Ohio State Reformatory shared her experience; "In the old Gym room, the floor was very bad. The people in the tour group were taking turns stepping in and out of the room to get to see it. When I stepped into that room, I saw a shadow man in the corner; however once again... there was no one there." **Cheyrl Kneram** related.

"It caught me off guard. I wasn't ready to see something like that and I will always remember how the hair on my arms and neck stood straight up. I saw a shadow. I saw a tall shadow. It came out of a cell and then it just vanished. I couldn't even breathe."-- **Paul Myers, Skeptic**

Shadow beings have also been described as forms of ghosts, demons, or even inter-dimensional beings. The most popular explanation seems to be that they are some sort of other dimensional beings whose dimension of origin occasionally overlaps with ours, which is said to explain their ethereal appearance and fleeting nature at times. There are "hatted" shadow beings, hooded shadows, cloaked ones, and solid or wispy, smoky types. Some are seen only from the waist up while others clearly have legs that are seen fleeing from their observers. They dart into corners, through solid walls, into closets, behind bushes, down hallways and around buildings. Sometimes they simply fade into the dark recesses of the night.

Those who are experiencing and studying the shadow people phenomenon say that these unique entities almost always used to be seen out of the corner of the eye and very briefly. But more and more, people are beginning to see them straight on and for longer periods of time. Some experiencers testify that they have even seen eyes (usually red) on these shadow beings.

The Ophiles's from Akron, Ohio met up with a shadow on their night at the Pen in 2009. Tim tells us about what he and wife Laura glimpsed. "As my wife and I were walking toward the wall, the shadow darted to our left of the exercise equipment. We shined our flashlights at the spot where we saw the shadow go and no one was there! As we got closer to the wall, the shadow darted back to where we first saw it appear. We chased the shadow for about 15-20 minutes before we got tired of trying to catch it. Finally, we walked up to where we first saw the shadow emerge from the door, only to find that there was no door there. It was a truly unique experience as we both felt that the shadow was playing games with us."

Bishop James Long, pastor of the St. Christopher Old Catholic Church in Louisville, Kentucky, has studied demonology for years and knows Shadow People well. He says that to him they are something evil. "Shadow People must be taken seriously and they can be quite dangerous," he said. "When a human spirit tries to manifest itself, its form is black, or otherwise known as Shadow. It is energy trying to manifest itself so that it can appear to have the physical characteristics it had when living on earth." These entities can move, communicate, and attack, drawing energy from their human victim. "Certainly Shadows that attack are demonic in nature and should be avoided at all times," Long said. "I would strongly encourage anyone who witnesses a dark Shadow to be careful."

In Islam, the supernatural Jinn can be a companion, or a dark, Shadowy predator. "Jinns are invisible entities believed in by most all Muslims and Middle Eastern folklore," said religion expert, Dashti Namaste. "Jinns get in and out of human spheres regularly, and it is believed that any human is able to make contact with a Jinn." Although Jinn can be benevolent, some Jinn are wicked, appearing as dark figures that lurk in ruins and cemeteries, waiting for an unsuspecting human soul to stumble by. The wicked Jinn, much like the demons of Christianity, are deceivers and may present themselves as the ghost of a loved one to insert themselves into a human's life. Clearly many religions and cultures have their own view on these entities.

Even before the Pen closed in 1995, inmates (and a few Correctional Officers and staff) spoke in hushed tones of spooky shadows that seem to flit across their cell walls. Vivid imaginations? Perhaps. But then again, maybe not. Of the thousands of people I have led down darkened hallways, shadow people seem to be a very common sighting. They are difficult to capture on film. The most famous photograph to date that I know of, is **Polly Gear's** photo of the "Shadow Man" that she captured in the cafeteria hallway at the Pen. I covered this in detail in *the Haunted History of the West Virginia Penitentiary* book but wanted to include a small portion of it here for new investigators to ponder over.

The following is Polly describing in her own words, what happened and how she captured the shadow man photograph. "The main experience that I had at the Pen was on the night of May 7th/8th in 2004 at 1:22 am. I was walking from the north yard area back inside through the cafeteria to go to the lobby for a break. As I walked through the small connector hallway and started down the main hallway to the lobby, I heard a metallic clang noise coming from the connector hall. This was a sound I had not heard before, so I walked back to the hallway and looked in, and saw, coming through the side wall of the door frame, a very black shadow of a man walking toward me, but it was looking out the windows onto the north yard. I could see the shadow man because of the light shining in the windows from the north yard. At this time, I realized that this was not a human, this was something paranormal. I then clicked on my flashlight and shined light onto this shadow person, I was amazed. I saw that the light was going right through it onto the wall behind it under the windows and the mass of it was very black moving static, such as you see on a TV set off cable. It was amazing to see this!"

"Shadow Man"© Photo by Polly Gear

Polly continues," I got a good look at it, as it was walking and looking out the windows, I had somewhat of a side view of it, it appeared to be only about two inches in thickness, and its movements were slightly animated, like it was walking fast, but wasn't actually moving as fast as it looked. At this point, the shadow man stopped because it had noticed that there was light shining on itself. It looked at its arm where my flashlight was on it. It looked up and around two times, then it saw me and it jumped behind the main hallway door frame. As the shadow man hid behind the door frame, I began to walk backwards away from it. I was going backwards down the main hall still facing the door where the shadow was. I was taking out my camera and turning it on. I wanted to try to get a photo of this entity."

"When the camera was ready, I stopped walking and held it out toward the door and took one photo. As the flash went off, I could see the shadow in the doorway. It had obviously stepped out to look at me at the same time I took the photo. The shadow instantly disappeared as the flash went off. I ran back to the area where it was and searched around. Nothing or anyone human was around the area. I then went to the lobby and showed the photo to the people in there. As recently as 2009, this photo and the camera have been analyzed by a forensic photographer. The camera was a Sony model Mavica CD 400. The photos are instantly burned on to a mini CD and the forensic photographer admits that the camera and the CD have not been tampered with and the photo has not been photo shopped or tampered with and that there IS mass to the figure of the shadow person ."

Polly further elaborates at the Angels & Ghosts website (www.angelsghosts.com) "I want to mention that on this night we had rented the penitentiary on a private basis and there were only 15 people there...and 13 of us were women. Neither of the two men there that evening were large men. They were men that I knew personally, so I know positively that I did not mistake this for a real person. I would also like to say that if I had any doubt at all about this photo being a real shadow person - one that I SAW with my own eyes at a distance of 10 feet, I would not have put this photo out in the public to be seen. I am showing this photo and telling my story of this experience and swear it to be truthful in my own words.

While walking the darkened hallways of the Pen and searching for proof of the afterlife pay attention to the shadows as well. Reports of shadow people have been around for centuries, but stories and sightings of these elusive entities are coming out now more than ever. In recent years, The Rhine Research Center (the Institute for Parapsychology) has gotten hundreds of reports from people claiming to have seen Shadow People. Paranormal research groups and "newbies" as well, are witnessing them during investigations, even being able to photograph some. What does this mean? Why are Shadow People being seen so much more now than in previous years? I think it is partly due to the fact that people are now a bit more aware of the paranormal and are more open to the subject than ever before.

Marc Cunningham, friend of the author and former Oho State Reformatory volunteer, had a glimpse of shadow people as well. He relates his details, "We went upstairs in the psych ward I think, I can't remember what it was, but it had a lot of glass around it. My friend and I hung out there and I know I kept seeing these black shapes moving out of the corner of my right eye. It would drive me crazy because as soon as I looked over there it would be gone."

So, we are still left with the question of what exactly is a shadow person. As with the paranormal subject in general, there seems to be more questions than answers. Most paranormal researchers do *agree* on one aspect, Shadow People are not human entities. I don't believe they're ghosts. I don't believe they're demons either. But, on a paranormal scale, I'd say Shadow People lean more towards the negative side, especially given the bad feelings I sometimes sense. Some researchers suggest that they're presence means something bad, or that something bad will soon happen. Some would say they are a harbinger of doom.

Whatever these entities are I am sure that as you explore the Pen you will take great care to watch where you walk...and will glance over your shoulder more than once at that "odd" shadow you thought you just saw.

CHAPTER 7
PSYCHIC IMPRESSIONS

One of the definitions of the word psychic explains "Psychic is a person who claims to have an ability to perceive information hidden from the normal senses through extrasensory perception (ESP), or who is said by others to have such abilities." There are also several different categories of psychic ability;

Clairvoyant Having: the supposed power to see objects or events that cannot be perceived by the senses. One of the most common abilities.

Clairaudient: The supposed power to hear things outside the range of normal perception. For instance, a clairaudient person might claim to hear the voices or thoughts of the spirits of persons who are deceased.

Clairalience: Also known as clairescence. In the field of parapsychology, clairalience is a form of extra-sensory perception wherein a person accesses psychic knowledge through the physical sense of smell. (ex. smelling a stench of burning flesh next to the electric chair.)

Clairgustance: In the field of parapsychology, clairgustance is defined as a form of extra-sensory perception that allegedly allows one to taste a substance without putting anything in one's mouth. It is claimed that those who possess this ability are able to perceive the essence of a substance from the spiritual or ethereal realms through taste. (ex. tasting blood when next to an area where a violent murder occurs)

Clairsentient: is a form of extra-sensory perception wherein a person acquires psychic knowledge primarily by feeling

Psychometry: Psychometry is related to clairsentience. The word stems from psyche and metric, which means "soul-measuring." Some psychics use the ability they have to touch or feel and object and relay what they feel to be the energy from previous owners. (ex. touching a scarf and being able to tell you about the woman who wore it.)

I think that many of us are a little bit psychic whether we acknowledge it or not. Every once in a while some of us get the feeling that the phone is going to ring... and then it does. Or perhaps know who it is that is calling and you are right. Or another instance is that a song is playing in your head; you turn on the radio, and there it is! The same song. Or perhaps you are thinking of someone you haven't seen in awhile and then when you are out at lunch- there they are.

Psychic impressions are many at the Pen. Multiple psychics have attended day tours or overnight hunts and many have had experiences ranging from feelings of dread, actual contact with prisoners from beyond or even being slapped such as the case of my friend Laura.

Laura Lyn is a wonderful person and a gifted Psychic Medium who lives in Ohio. Her website is www.angelreader.net. She and I have worked on many cases together and I consider her a valuable asset to any investigation. Laura's first visit to the Pen left an impression on both of us. I recall that we were doing the walk around tour right before our overnight ghost hunt began. We had walked into the contact visitation room where happy murals of cartoon characters are painted on the walls. This was to make it seem "friendly" to families visiting loved ones incarcerated. Laura was backed up against a wall next to me listening to the tour guide. Suddenly Laura leaned over to me and whispered with a bit of panic in her tone "There's a man in here by the name of Buddy who doesn't like women!" and as I looked at her in the dim light of the room she flinched a bit and started to point to her cheek. "My cheek is burning like I've been slapped!" she said. (We tried to do this quietly as others were beginning to look at us in the shadows) I shined my small flashlight up at her face and noticed a creeping redness across her cheek. I think it left a lasting impression on us in that room. Just because it 'looked' like a happy spot, didn't mean that it *was*. The room we were in was the old cafeteria area where the 1986 riot began.

Laura's abilities definitely aid her during investigations as she says she can "see ghosts, feel and hear energy." Her first impression of the Pen was as follows, "I was very impressed with the energy. I saw more ghosts in the West Virginia Pen than in any other area. In my opinion the West Virginia Penitentiary is among the most haunted locations across the nation." I asked her to explain any activity she experiences, if any and this was her reply, "I was most impressed by the yard. I used the ghost communicator all through the pen and I was amazed by the activity in the yard. I never heard so much cussing in my life!!! The FCC would have banned any broadcasts that would have put out the words we were all hearing over the radio through the ghost box. The ghosts were having a lot of fun cussing all of us out."

On a more serious note Laura adds, "There is an ominous figure that looms in the Sugar Shack. I have not captured his name; he isn't at all interested to talk with me. He shows himself as a dark rather large energy that has a habit of grunting and growling. I think he is actually several energies that have combined forces. Like a collective dark mass with intelligence and anger."

Susan Sheppard is the creator of "The Phoenix Cards, a past-life deck", the "Astrological Guide to Seduction & Romance", "Cry of the Banshee", and the "Gallows Tree", a novel. She is the creator and tour guide for the Haunted Parkersburg Ghost Tours in Parkersburg, West Virginia and has published other books in addition to those listed above.

I knew Susan had to have experienced something in the Pen and I was right. "I was choked in Red Snyder's cell and also outside the boiler room where the one prisoner was murdered." Susan continued with her tale, "I could tolerate the slight choking, and it didn't scare me, but there was definite pressure placed on the front of my throat which tightened. Still I could breathe and the pressure vanished when I left the area. In the Sugar Shack, I saw several, small demons near the floor dragging themselves around by front legs or "arms." They resembled dark red, mucous-covered frogs without any back legs. They reminded me of creatures from a Hieronymus Bosch painting."
 You can access Susan's website here:
http://users.wirefire.com/magick/new_page_6.htm

Debra Robinson lives in New Philadelphia, Ohio with her husband Rod. Talk about a creative streak! Debra is a Psychic, palm reader and musician. Debra has been to the Pen on four occasions for overnight investigations in 2007, 2008, 2009, and 2011.

I asked her to explain her ability and how she came across knowing she possessed them. Debra says, "I have seen them, occasionally hear them; sometimes am given information from them if they decide to tell me something meant as a message for someone else; I am clairvoyant, clairaudient, clairsentient; the modern names for my abilities, (we used to call them telepathy, precognition, etc.) and various other things, and I was born with them, and some say I may have inherited them from my Mother and Grandmother, who also had them." Her initial impression of the Pen? "Dark, massive & forbidding!"

I asked Debra if she believed the Pen was haunted or paranormal active and if so, what kind of experiences did she have? Debra says "I absolutely believe it is active, no doubt at all. The most active area for me is the first hallway after leaving the visitor center, Red's cell area, the Alamo section in North Hall, there are just so many really awful feeling places, the atmosphere is so thick you could cut it with a knife, it's pretty brutal for anyone with any psychic ability at all, almost unbearable at times. It's the kind of place you feel oppressed, and threatened, and in danger of being attacked."
Check out Debra's website www.psychicdebra.net

Sheri Claire's occupation is that of full-time Clairvoyant and Medium. Sheri lives in Columbus, Ohio and ventured to the WV Pen on two separate instances. "I had been invited to join a professional ghost hunting team that was visiting the WV Pen on a previous occasion. Because experiencing the presence of spirits on a regular basis was not unfamiliar to me, I was curious to see if my experience would be different in a setting that is notoriously known for being "haunted". To my surprise, the recognition of spirit activity was not all that different overall. What was dramatically different for me was what I experienced more in a clairvoyant sense. The structure of the WV Pen itself is impressive. As the actual building comes into sight, it has a dramatic presence of its own. Our group arrived in the evening, after dark. As soon we pulled into the parking spaces located directly in front of the building I felt a heaviness that was palpable. I immediately started receiving images so rapidly that it literally took me some time to process. When I stepped out of the vehicle it intensified. What I was struck with was the feeling of violence, sadness, anger. I would even venture to say a hint of hopelessness. It was quite overwhelming. Once I became adjusted to the environment. I was able to tune in more clearly to the various energies that are residing at the Pen. "

Sheri tells us of her second visit to the gothic fortress, "Later, I was again invited to join a friend for another tour of the Pen. He too, was interested in attempting to collect photographs and quantifiable measurements and data during our visit. The hope was that I would be able to use my abilities to direct him to the most effective locations and best timing for capturing some form of activity. Because I had been there previously, I felt I could navigate better on this particular visit."

I asked Sheri to explain the events that occurred on the night she investigated with us at the WV Pen on September 18, 2010. She had a great memory for detail as many investigators do. Sheri elaborated on her night investigation, "As I mentioned before, I felt slightly more prepared for this visit, as I had been there once before. I enjoyed the tour that was given at the beginning of the evening. I found this to be a good time for me to feel out the Pen that night. Generally, I am pulled to more active areas. In the case of mediumship, which involves direct spirit communication, I am sometimes drawn by a specific entity that may want my attention. Often when a spirit recognizes that a medium can communicate with him or her, it is a bit like a moth to a flame. I found this to be true in a number of places within the Pen. During the tour, I was drawn to a particular cell located on the second floor. I remember asking my friend to make note of the cell number and location so we could return to it later in the evening. As it turns out, we did return there. Not only did I pick up on a presence there immediately and was able to communicate with him, but also my friend was able to capture what looks like mist just outside of that particular cell in that very moment. This "mist" only appears in one or two of the photos he took in sequential order at that time. I also felt a physical touch in my hair. The photos show the "mist" extending to my hair."

Sheri continues, "After the tour was completed, we were allowed to explore the area on our own. During this time, Sherri Brake was kind enough to escort me down to the boiler room. This is a relatively small area, comparably speaking. While we were down there, Sherri gave a brief history and asked what I was picking up if anything. Because I am very sensitive to energy, I often like to walk the perimeter of a room and will sometime literally use my hand to feel the energy while I am picking up information. I first began to get some details about the inmate that was contained in that area. I felt his emotion. I felt him feeling fiercely defensive and protective. Some of the visions I received were quite graphic and violent. I also got the sense of being chased or moving about the room."

"As I was verbalizing much of this, there were two men sitting quietly in the room listening. They were also there for the tour that evening. I began to pick up a male spirit that wanted my attention. He kept mentioning to me that his family was there. I assumed at that time, that he was referring to family in the past. I also heard what sounded like the name "Matt". I was communicating this, and he became more persistent about his family. One of the two men sitting in the dark spoke up, and said, "What did you say? Did you say he said he has family here?" When I replied yes, this opened up a dialogue, and "Matt" the spirit, began to figuratively pull me outside. He was asking me to follow him. Then men stood, and shared with me that they were actual blood relatives to a man that had been an inmate there named, "Matt". Not knowing exactly where I was heading, I allowed myself to be pulled. The two men, Sherri, my friend and I walked up the stairs and around to the left. We walked alongside an outdoor, fenced in basketball court. When I arrived at the outer corner I stopped abruptly, and said, "Here. He is stopping here. This is where he wants to talk to you." In that moment, I did not understand why this location held significance for him. He then began to show me his execution and the moments leading up to it. He wanted the family to know he was grateful they were there. He began to tell me how he felt his family had abandoned him in shame, and he showed me his loneliness there. Sherri then reveals to us that this location, which now appeared as an outdoor court, was actually the former location of the Death House where executions took place. This, indeed, was where this man had lost his life."

Sheri mentions where she felt the most activity that night, "I found the outdoor yard to be quite active. I could actually see men in clusters there. I could feel a lot of small groups gathering there. We were able to capture what appear to be orbs in a number of photographs. One experience that stands out for me actually occurred on my initial visit. A group of us were standing in the middle of a line of cells in the North Hall when we suddenly heard a very loud slam of a cell door. There was no mistaking the sound. It was so loud I literally jumped and let out a scream. We immediate rushed down to the end to examine the area. Every cell door was open." Visit her website at www.shericlaire.com

Many other psychics have toured the prison after its closing in 1995 and the majority of them have had experiences that would leave many of us scratching our head in amazement. While some nights at the prison are paranormally quieter than other nights, it's always a gamble when you roll the dice as a ghost hunter. You never know what you are going to get.

You don't have to be psychic to have a "encounter'. Use your own senses and abilities. Find a quiet spot and just sit. Turn on your voice recorder and ask some questions while trying your hand at Electronic Voice Phenomena or the capture of spirit voices. I particularly encourage you to try this out in North Hall or upstairs in the Psych ward or Medical infirmary. There have been fantastic captures of voices in those locations.

Some people believe we all have psychic abilities as I think we do. Some of us may have more natural abilities than others, the same way that some of us seem inclined towards music or mathematics. But just like any other skill, psychic abilities can be trained and enhanced.

How can you enhance or work on your ability? Experiment with various techniques until you find one that feels right for you. Meditation is thought to greatly help. Remember, there is no right way or wrong way to perform meditation. It is only important that you are able to relax and focus your mind. If you continue the practice of meditation for any length of time, you will begin to notice the existence of your own spiritual energy. It is the connection to your spiritual self which helps provides intuitive information. Strengthening the connection to your spiritual self will result in an increase of your own psychic abilities Meditation is most important for psychic abilities. It can help you in many walks of life-for instance.

Try to be more aware of your surroundings. Upon waking in the morning, make an effort to lie still for a few minutes without opening your eyes. Try to notice as many sounds and smells as possible before you decide to open your eyes. This exercise, if carried out for several weeks, can greatly help to increase your levels of awareness and intuition. Give it a try. I don't suggest trying this while lying in a cell at the prison though. You could really scare someone to death if they walked in there thinking it was empty!

Listen. The act of listening is important in increasing your psychic awareness. After continuing this exercise for some time, you will begin to notice an increase in your overall awareness, which affects your level of intuition. It takes patience so practice, practice, practice.

Pay attention to random thoughts and feelings. Keep a journal handy at all times and try to write down those thoughts that seem to come out of nowhere. Try keeping it in your night stand next to your bed. You may notice after a while that some patterns tend to emerge. Thoughts that previously seemed completely random and unconnected begin to form themes or recognizable ideas.

Record your dreams in your journal. If you have been following the awareness exercise outlined above you will have noticed that your dreams are much easier to recall. Allowing yourself a few minutes to be still upon waking makes it much easier to remember dreams and with more detail than if you rush out of bed in the morning and hurry to start the day. Try setting your alarm clock to wake you up ten or fifteen minutes before your normal waking time. Give yourself some time to remember your dreams and make notes.

Good locations in the Pen to work with your intuition

- Medical Infirmary/Psych Ward

On the second floor of the building you will find the medical infirmary area and the psychiatric area. These are typically quieter areas in the Pen and perfect places to sit on the floor and use your intuition. Be quiet; absorb the sounds of the area, the feel of the floor and the smells around you. Let your mind wander a bit and see what you feel or visualize.

The hallway of the Medical Infirmary
Photo by Perry Queener

- The Exercise Yard or Bullpen Area

This is located outside and I would suggest you wait till the yard is empty of anyone else. Find the area where you see the basketball hoops. Walk inside the area and stand on the pavement. You are now standing where the Death House once stood. Close your eyes and be still. Think of the men who were executed on that very site and what they may have felt or thought before they left this dimension. Take notes and put down on paper your thoughts or feelings. Some investigators have had the feelings of static electricity on their hands while standing here. One even mentioned to me she smelled burning flesh. I cannot even imagine.

- North Hall

No other area in the building saw as much violence then the North Hall which is located on the first floor. Sound can tend to echo here so be very careful before you begin your experiment. Walk down the length of cells and pay attention to your feelings.

North Hall
Photo by the Author 2012

When you are "drawn" into a cell or feel compelled to walk into one for some reason, sit down on the bunk and listen. Listen for human voices. If you do not hear anyone, chances are you have picked a good time to try this exercise. Take your flashlight and look at the wall. Hopefully, you remembered to bring one! Use your cell phone light if you did not. Read the graffiti on the walls. Most cells have something scribbled down whether it be scratched into the metal or written by marker. Prisoners would decorate their cells this way, sometimes by doing it as a journal, a quote they liked, a song lyric etc.. This gives you a glimpse into who occupied the cell at one time. Put your hand on the drawing or words and close your eyes. What do you feel? Any emotions come to surface? A name? Sadness? Hate? Sit back down and jot these down. Especially if a name came to your mind. Be sure to note the cell number or location so you can ask staff about it later.

Sugar Shack Mothman Paintings
Not painted by inmates but by MTV. This was done without permission. Photo from Author's collection 2009

- Sugar Shack

The Sugar Shack is a legendary spot for ghost hunters. This was the indoor recreation room. As you walk down the steps into the area, be careful as they are uneven and it can throw your perception off a bit. Turn to the right at the bottom of the steps and walk towards the doorway. Step into the big room. You are now in the Sugar Shack. NO murders occurred here although some popular TV shows tell you differently. There were physical attacks made though and some sexual activity was said to occur as well, hence the name "Sugar Shack". Turn off your flashlights. Lean up against a wall. It's easier to be steady that way in complete darkness. Listen carefully for whispers (right next to you) as many have heard them Also be aware that the lobby is directly above you so if you hear people talking above you or toilets flushing....they are in THIS dimension. Let your eyes get accustomed to the darkness. Look in the corners of the room from where you stand. An image of a man with a shovel was seen here by guide Lori O'Neil and her husband one evening. He disappeared before their very eyes. Feel the atmosphere in this room. Sometimes it is "light" and other times it will feel "heavy". This is a great place to explore but try to be the only one here if you can. You may have to wait awhile if there is a large group present on your tour or overnight hunt.

Many psychics have told me that *accepting* you may have these abilities is the very first step. Develop them. Practice your meditation and record it in your dream journal. Look around locally and see if there are any reputable instructors who hold classes on developing intuition. Good luck!

CHAPTER 8
THE GEAR

When I began investigating nearly 30 years ago, all I used was a camera. It was pretty light packing up for an investigation. Just film, yes...35mm film, my camera and a flashlight and I was good for the night. Speed ahead to the year 2003 and I found myself packing a large case of equipment and donning a photographer's vest with about 25 pockets. Seriously! Here is a list of basic equipment you can purchase or bring to your investigation.

Air Ion Counter: This device measures positive and negative ions in the air. Ghosts can cause a lot of positive ions because they give off high amounts of electromagnetic discharges. However the price can be high, around $400 - $600. Ouch. I do not have one but felt compelled to list it here.

Batteries: Many ghost hunters have noted (and have been frustrated by the fact) that haunted and active locations tend to drain batteries. Even new and fresh batteries seem to go dead quickly. So this is even more reason to make sure you have plenty on hand.

Cameras: There many to choose from and various price points. Whatever brand you pick get to know it like the back of your hand and keep the lens clean, clean, clean. Nothing is worse than stopping an investigation to get the book out on how to use that new camera you bought on the way to the hunt. Suggestions: Digital; Canon EOS rebel XTi, Fuji S5000, Vivitar 3675, Samsung Digimax A402. SLR models would be Minolta XG-7 or the Nikon F3. Can you use your cell phone camera? I wouldn't recommend it. Cell phone cameras are not adequate, even if they have a 5 megapixel or higher resolution. The image sensors in cell phones are too small and the lenses are not very good.

Cassette Recorders: I am old school. Yes, I still carry around an old fashioned tape recorder that takes cassette tapes. They are a dying breed, I know! Use them to record EVP. Although nothing may be heard during the investigation there is a phenomenon called EVP (electronic voice phenomenon) whereby spirit voices have been known to appear on tape later after being reviewed. Ensure the use of brand new tapes when recording. Don't use old ones as you can have bleed thru.

Compasses: Nice, cheap tool to have. A compass is not only very useful for navigation it is also great for picking up electromagnetic forces. A compass will react to any magnetic or electrical stimulus that may be out of the ordinary. For this reason it is probably better to avoid an electronic compass instead use the needle point's north kind.

Computers/Laptops: A must have for Electronic Voice Phenomena and photo editing. Comes in handy for documenting investigations but I strongly suggest a paper back up. Think of the 100s of hours of work you have into investigations. It would be a shame to lose all of that documentation in a computer crash.

Digital Voice Recorders: For collection of EVP's and note taking. An invaluable source to have. Again, get the best one you can afford because the higher the price, the better the quality. You'll want a model that can record high-quality sound. Some of the more expensive models record in uncompressed modes, which gives you the best fidelity. Suggestions: RCA, Olympus.

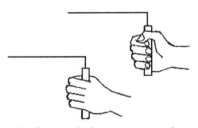

L shaped dowsing rods

Dowsing Rods: Simple instrument to make and to use. 90% of people have the ability to do this. Dowsing is where quantum physics meets with mysticism, still impossible to measure with scientific instruments, only accessible to our intuition. Imagine a device where pendulum type movement in the hand of a dowser is an equivalent of a needle on an EMF meter used to measure subtle energy not detected by other senses. You can make two L shaped rods from clothes hangers. Hold them in your hands and think of "spirit or ghosts" and they will possibly move to show you where energy is at. Begin your investigation in that area. Dowsing is a complex field and can be very rewarding when done correctly.

EMF meters: For detecting electromagnetic fields you would use one these handy dandy meters. If you have ever watched any of the television shows showing investigators doing their thing, you have probably seen one! As the name suggests, this device detects electromagnetic fields. There is a theory that spirits can cause fluctuation in EMF's, so an unexplainable high spike could possibly be linked to paranormal phenomena. Suggestions: Gaussmaster, Cell Sensor, KII meter, Trifield Natural EM, Trifield 100EX. Mel meter REM-ATDD model features simultaneous EMF, EM Field output, temp alert with illuminated display and flashlight. 1 Axis Gaussmaster is great as it ignores manmade energy fields such as 60 Hz magnetic fields and runs about $170 (a great place for EMF meters is www.lessemf.com)

Infrared Thermometers: For instant readings of extreme temperature fluctuations. Infrared light is part of the electromagnetic spectrum. It falls between visible light and radio waves. Every object can reflect, transmit and emit energy. Emitted energy can indicate the temperature of that certain object. In investigations of the paranormal, cold spots can be a common anomaly. It is thought and believed by many, that an entity can use the energy of a certain location to try to manifest itself. When this occurs, it creates a cold mass. This type of energy is not seen with the human eye but it can be detected by using a device like an IR thermometer.

Be sure to get one that has a backlit display for use in complete darkness. Suggestions: La Crosse Technology

Infrascan model # IR-101, RadioShack wireless Infrared and the Cen-Tech Non-Contact Infrared Thermometer with Laser Targeting. (great deals at Harbor Freight!)

Laser Grid: Have you ever caught movement on your camera and you can't quite make out its shape or whether it even has a mass to it? Using a laser grid helps determine both. It's best to place a laser grid in front of a running camera throughout the investigation. (if you can) Upon your review, if movement happens it will be apparent by the breaking of the laser pattern. You can go frame by frame in the video marking where the pattern shifts thereby drawing an outline shape of the entity itself. If the pattern moves a certain way you can even determine if the entity has 3-dimensional mass and map that as well. Pretty cool, eh?
Suggestions: Laser Grid Scope - This high powered laser emits a grid of green dots useful for detecting shadows or general visual disturbances during an investigation.

Mel Meter: When you need to measure EMF and temperature, you need one hand operation that gives you a wealth of information, and lots of options. Investigators love a tool that can do two things at once.

This device offers both single axis AC Magnetic field measurement and real time air temperature readings Readout is in mG or °F or °C. High resolution and a very fast response. Basic 1 inch K-Type thermocouple is included and it can be used with a variety of commercially available thermocouple probes for extended temperature ranges. Solves the age old paranormal equipment problem of "How do I hold all this stuff?" Seriously!

There is an interesting story behind the development of this tool. The Mel Meter was designed and developed by Gary Galka of DAS Distribution Inc. Gary lost one of his three daughters, Melissa. After Melissa's sudden passing in a car accident, some incredible things started to happen to him and his family. Melissa began to make her presence known through numerous ADC's (after death communications) to Gary and his family. Gary designed the Mel Meter as a way to communicate with his daughter whom Gary says helped with the healing process.

The flagship device in the line of Mel Meters is the Mel-8704-SB7-EMF meter, which detects a range of electromagnetic and temperature changes, has an AM/FM scanner, includes glow-in-the-dark buttons, and includes an "exclusive P-SB7 Integrated Sprit Box".

Equipment usually drains quickly but this Mel Meter isn't too bad. Expect about 15 hours with the back lit display on and 40 hours if the back lit display light is off.

Motion Detectors: These devices are good for sensing movement when there should be none. One sensor can easily monitor an entire hallway or room. It is an ideal tool for indoor investigations. Motion detection works for remotely located rooms (400 foot range max). Most alarms sound if an object detectable by infrared passes by the sensor. Some models are equipped with cameras and will snap a picture.

These sensors are calibrated so that the object must be somewhat sizable to set it off -- a mouse or a bug passing by won't trigger it. I would not recommend using this at the Pen for an investigation but perhaps at a private home.

Nite Vision: This device is similar to combining a video camera with a night vision scope and allows the recording of light not normally visible to the naked eye. Night Vision scopes can be very useful. Cheap night vision adapters are available that will attach the scopes to video cameras for about $30. However Night Vision Equipment can be expensive. Choose monocular or binocular equipment. Binocular are a good choice because they add the benefit of depth perception. Prices range between $250-$4000. You can get some good scopes in the $300 range that work well on video equipment.

Ovilus: A somewhat newer item gaining popularity in the field. The Ovilus is an electronic speech-synthesis device which utters words depending on environmental readings, including electromagnetic waves. The Ovilus has an embedded database of words. It contains an EMF Meter, among several other environmental sensors. These readings are combined to create a number, and this number is used to reference the database of words. The Ovilus then "speaks" that word. An Ovilus can also operate in a phonetic mode that reacts to EMF variations to create words that are not in the database. There are other types of the Ovilus device out there, including the Paranormal Puck, Video Ovilus, Ovilus I, Ovilus II, Ovilus FX, and Ovilus X. I urge you to be cautious when using equipment such as this that can generate any word and was manufactured as an entertainment device, not a true paranormal tool.

Pendulum Dowsing: Basic dowsing is asking questions and getting answers determined by a certain kind of movement of a dowsing pendulum. Dowsing is the ability of seeking answers and interpreting them. You can use an actual pendulum or even use a necklace with a medallion or hang a washer on a string. Pendulums such as a crystal can used as well and are perhaps the most common. The user first determines which direction (left-right or up-down) will indicate "yes" and which "no" before proceeding to ask the pendulum specific questions. The person holding the pendulum try's to hold it as steadily as possible. An interviewer may pose questions to the person holding the pendulum, and it swings by minute unconscious bodily movement in the direction of the answer. Give it a try!

Thermal Cameras: We all have probably seen these in use on any one of the ghost hunting shows on television. Thermal Imaging Cameras are used to help provide evidence of the paranormal field by detecting energy (heat) which the human eye may not be able to see. Another theory is that since ghosts may contain energy, they will in return have heat. Cold spot theory is another one that suggests that these entities absorb energy around them to manifest themselves which in turn create a cold spot in that area. Disadvantages: Pricey. Only able to detect surface temperatures. Accurate temperature measurements are hindered by reflections from other surfaces
Advantages to thermography:
- It shows a visual picture so temperatures over a large area can be compared
- It is capable of catching moving targets in real time
- It can be used to measure or observe in areas inaccessible or hazardous for other methods
- It is a non-destructive test method
- It can be used to detect objects in dark areas

Two Way Radios: These devices allow you to communicate with your ghost hunting party. If you are investigating a house and you have people scattered all over, walkie-talkies allow you to keep in touch. Disadvantages; can interfere and contaminate EVP sessions.

Video: All cameras can be used remotely and monitored via the lobby or wherever you want your "base camp" to be. This is better used if you have a private hunt at the Pen and have the place ALL to yourself! The wireless IR camera provides a live feed when carried through an investigation by a team member. All cameras have low light or total darkness capabilities with IR. Video is a great asset to have to either carry with you or to set up on a tripod and let it run in hopes of catching something anomalous.

The choices with video these days are simply amazing. Get the very best one you can afford. High-definition video has become quite affordable, and it's advantageous to get a camera that has either an internal hard drive or that can record on memory cards. These allow you to easily transfer your video to a computer for editing and analysis. Suggestions: Sony TRV-118 Hi8 w/ IR Night Shot, JVC GR SXM 740 Night Alive VHS-C, DXG 301V and Sony HVL-IRM IR video light

Various equipment
Photo from Authors collection

Accouterments and extras: backpack or case for equipment, photographers vest to hold items, extra batteries for flashlights and other equipment, extra media storage cards, tripods for cameras, extra camera lenses and filters, bug repellent, extension cords and cables, trigger objects, notepad/paper pen/first aid kit/ID/small tool kit/battery tester.

In conclusion I would like to state that equipment is only as good as the operator. Learn your equipment inside and out. Know what battery type it takes, how to change them and what its limits are. You can spend all the money in the world on a piece of expensive equipment but if you don't know how to turn it on well….you might as well stayed home from the hunt!

Some investigators theorize that too much equipment takes away from the actual investigation and this makes sense. If you are busy lugging around cases of equipment, checking your battery juice, looking for those cables you packed SOMEWHERE, you are out of the "zone" and can miss a subtle paranormal event. Some folks think less is best. You decide. Maybe a happy medium?

CHAPTER 9
PARANORMAL HOTSPOTS

Each location is unique, of course. Many buildings only give you a slight glimpse of activity while others are just simply "quiet". Some locations are full of paranormal energy and oddities while offering episodes of activity that continually entice those to explore the shadows for evidence, time and time again. If you are a paranormal researcher or investigator then you know what I am speaking about. Activity can happen daytime or nighttime. I. like many of you, prefer to investigate at night. Equipment reads better with the backlights and it is generally a quiet atomhosphere to investigate in. Traffic and humans voices outside of buildings will be quieter which aids in an investigation.

At the Penitentiary in Moundsville, any area can offer up a paranormal occurrence. We have had paranormal oddities happen in the lobby area. A Dan, one of out bus drivers for our overnight tours, heard a voice behind him and he was the only one in the lobby at that time!

I've listed some of the areas in the Penitentiary that you should investigate, time allowing. Some are off of the beaten path so be sure to take the extra time to visit them.

1st Floor:

Contact visitation room: As you exit the lobby to go inside of the Pen, turn to your left. Walk around the corner and you will see a door that opens into a large room. You can't miss this room because there are multiple paintings on the wall. Mutant Ninja Turtles, a wizard and a log cabin complete with black bear adorn the room. This is where the 1986 riot began on New Year's Day. This riot killed three inmates and sixteen employees were taken hostage.

Contact Visitation room
Photo by the Author 2010

This was the old cafeteria area and is one of the area's most people do not bother to investigate for some reason. Maybe it's the cartoon figures painted on the wall that tends to give you the impression it's a "happy" place? Don't neglect this area. Psychic Medium Laura Lyn was harassed by an entity named Buddy. She was smacked by his energy right on the side of her face. It was enough to leave a very large reddened area. (I was a witness to this) Multiple EVPS have been captured in here and many solid, glowing orb anomalies captured. (be sure it's not dust!)

Cafeteria Hallway: This is where the infamous Shadow Man photograph was captured by Polly Gear. As you leave the lobby area, go thru the secured doors and turn to your left. Follow the hallway around and you will see a long hallway over 100 feet long. This is the hallway. Walk down the hall till you are standing in front of the Cafeteria door. It is marked "Cafeteria". This is where the shadow was captured at. Be sure to take some photographs here.

The Cafeteria Hallway
Photo by Author 2007

Cafeteria: When TAPS Ghost hunters filmed here back in 2006, they had some experiences in the kitchen ar5ea but it never made it to the final cut for airing on the show. Don't pass this area up. Watch out for the gas lines and other obstacles as you walk thru there in the dark.

The large Cafeteria area
Photo by Author 2007

North Hall: Not only was this the area where the worst of the worst were sent to, but it is probably one of the most active areas. Suicides by hanging, stabbing and murders occurred in this cell block area. North Hall is accessed from the inside of the Pen by walking down past the Cafeteria door continuing on past the "Wheel".

The Wheel is a large apparatus that inmates entered when they first arrived at the Pen. It could be spun by the guard in any direction allowing security for the Warden whose residence and offices were upstairs. GO past the Wheel and proceed down a couple of steps. You will see a lot of fencing and a few picnic tables. This is North Hall, also called The Alamo.

North Hall, the Alamo
Photo by Author 2005

There are gun aisles opposite the tiers which also have wire fencing. The cells on the lower tiers are also 5 by 7 feet, with crutch keys used to lock the doors. The walls are steel with concrete floor on the lower level and steel floors on the upper tiers. The doors are small and narrow with bars covered by mesh. Many visitors have mentioned feeling like a caged animal as they explore here for the first time.

This are is a hotbed of activity. If you sit down at the picnic tables you are sitting in an area where a paranormal photo was captured during a day tour.

Photo from the MEDC collection

Debra Robinson, psychic and palm reader says this of North Hall, "the Alamo section in North Hall, there are just so many really awful feeling places, the atmosphere is so thick you could cut it with a knife, it's pretty brutal for anyone with any psychic ability at all, almost unbearable at times. It's the kind of place you feel oppressed, and threatened, and in danger of being attacked." (www.psychicdebra.net)

Red Snyder's Cell, North Hall "B" side:

Walk through the area in North Hall with the picnic tables and go off to the right side. You can walk past an area of cells. The cells doors should be on your left. If you enter any of these ground level cells, turn on your recorders and try to capture some EVP. If you walk all the way down to the end of the row, you will find yourself at the last cell on the left which is one of the most talked about prisoners, Red Snyder. You will know you are in Red's cell when you see the graffiti. It says *Aryan Brotherhood* scrawled on the right side of the cell wall as you enter. One bunk in on the left. People have become light headed and even fainted in this cell. I had my hair tugged on two separate occasions in this cell. EVPs recorded have been on the negative side.

Red Snyder's cell in North Hall
Photo by Author

William Andrew "Red" Snyder was born on December 26th 1946, the day after Christmas. He was born in Weston, West Virginia and was sent to the Pen for 1st degree murder of his father and a neighbor in 1968. His education consisted of completing the seventh grade before he became inmate # 45512. He was brutally murdered in December of 1992 by another inmate.

Red, as he was commonly known due to his red hair, was both liked and feared by prison staff. He was 5 feet 8 inches tall with hazel eyes according to his mug shot record and his occupation was listed as a laborer.

It says "Aryan Brotherhood" scrawled on the right side as you enter. One bunk in on the left. People have become light headed and even fainted in this cell. I had by hair tugged on two separate occasions in this cell. EVPs recorded have been on the negative side.

William "Red" Snyder
Photo from the MEDC collection

"He was just funny," Maggie Gray says. Maggie is a retired Correctional Officer and worked at the Pen when Red was incarcerated. "He'd talk to me about 'Days of Our Lives' as if those people lived just next door." "But if he told you he was going to kill you," she says, "that's exactly what he meant." Snyder was housed in the North Hall cell block, an area for misfits and particularly violent inmates. North Hall's Alamo section totaled 98 cells and 4 tiers. "B" side housed the most violent ones, the ones who could not play nicely with others. The "worst of the worst" were housed here and stayed in their cell 23 hours per day. Red wasn't sent to North Hall immediately upon being imprisoned. He was in the mainline section until he stabbed another inmate in 1971. That event earned him a trip to North Hall where he stayed until his violent murder occurred in 1992. To be sent to North Hall meant you did something terrible after you were in the prison. Some called it the "prison within a prison". In an October 1976 newspaper, Warden McKenzie said of North Hall, "This is where we house the incorrigibles. Anyone who makes life miserable for other inmates goes there."

Red Snyder would have been a candidate for the electric chair if the death penalty hadn't been abolished in 1965.

Paranormal activity: How does it feel for you to be in Red's cell? Those who are sensitive or psychic have felt his presence there on many occasions. EVPS are popular in this cell with one coming to mind that was captured by a female police officer on a ghost hunt. "Not so fast" was the ghostly sentence uttered. One male sensitive actually fainted while being in the cell that features "Aryan Nation" on its wall graffiti. (Red was a member) Be sure to take some time in this cell. It's worth it.

Step out of Red's cell and turn to your right and walk down two cells. Russell Lassiter occupied this cell at one time.

Rusty Lassiter's cell, North Hall "B" side:

Lassiter was born August of 1956 and had been a bar manager when he was arrested and convicted of 1st degree murder and malicious wounding. He was 25 years old when he was admitted to the Pen for his crime and became inmate # 49386. He brutally killed Red Snyder in 1992 after rushing towards him near his cell. A 6 foot and 2 inch tall inmate came at a 5 feet 8 inch inmate and within seconds, nearly 40 stab wounds were inflicted with a piece of shank.

Rusty, unfortunately is no stranger to prison life at this time. He is currently incarcerated in St. Mary's Correctional Facility with a scheduled parole hearing January 1, 2105.

Russell Lassiter
From the West Virginia DOC website

Walk past Red Snyder's cell and to the end of the cell block. Turn left and walk a step or two and stop. You are in an area that once housed a cell. The cell is no longer there but if you look closely, you can make out where it was connected. This is where cell 22 was located. (on A side) A young man by the name of Eddie Fielder hung himself.

Cell #20, North Hall "A" side
You are now in the "A" side of North Hall. Walk to cell #20 and go inside. You have entered the cell of a self-proclaimed Satanist. This inmate was housed in this cell in the mid 1970's and actually escaped from the Pen 3 times. (and was brought back each time!) He would sit in his cell

and try to summon Satan. I wrote about this inmate in great detail in my book, *"The Haunted History of the West Virginia Penitentiary."*

In my book, he spoke of his darker days, "I took chicken bones from our meals and hung them on my walls. I drew the face of Satan on a sheet and hung it from my ceiling in my cell. I made a pentagram on a pillow case and put it on my floor. All the little things that I could do with the information that I got from the pamphlet I had ordered while in the Pen. It was a pamphlet from Anton LaVey." (Author's note: Anton Szandor LaVey was the founder of the Church of Satan. He was the author of The Satanic Bible)

I would suggest trying your hand at dowsing in this cell. See what energy you can find. Interested in one way that this inmate escaped? Look on the wall below the vent. See the outline of a rectangle? This inmate starved himself and covered his body in butter so that he could slip into this section he cut out with shank. Can you even imagine?

If you are interested in this former prisoners story, his DVD is for sale in the lobby gift shop or you can order it below. This former inmate became a minister and brings youth groups to the Pen to warn them of life's bad choices.

To purchase John Verton's "Choices" pamphlet or his DVD, "Executive Clemency" go online at www.bcaministries.com. They can be purchased by calling the church at (304) 853 - 2077
Burnsville Church of the Apostles
PO Box 515
Burnsville, WV 26335

Cell# 2, North Hall "A" side

As you exit cell #20, turn to your left and walk down towards the end of the cells. Stop at cell #2. You will know you have arrived when you look inside and see the popular red lips and tongue artwork familiar with the Rolling Stone's band.

Danny Lehman, inmate #48891, was from Raleigh County, West Virginia and was housed in North Hall. He was a talented painter and some of his work is still present on the walls of the Pen. Unusual photographs captured in this cell with unexplained shadows and mists. High EMF readings on many occasions. (no electric in the cells)

Lehman helped during the riot of 1986 as it was quickly agreed upon (by the inmates) as he was best suited for the task of negotiating with authorities during the riot. He did help to present the demands of the inmates to the media. Yet, Lehman was not a part of the twenty men who began the riot on January 1st.

Danny was stabbed through the eye as he returned to his cell following a recreation period on November 28, 1986. He was declared brain dead a few days later on Friday November 28th and died later that day.

Danny Lehman

Danny Lehman's cell. Photo by the Author 2007

North Recreation Yard/the Bull Pen area:

Leave North Hall area and walk outside into the yard. See the enclosed area with basketball hoops surrounded by stainless steel razor wire? This exercise area was the location of the Death House where the majority of the executions took place.

The Death House was a building that was built in 1899 at the cost of $6000 dollars. It was two stories tall and was made of brick and stone. It was home to nearly all of the executions. (Some say the Wagon Gate was the site of the first executions with first one being Shep Caldwell in 1899) 94 executions took place at the Penitentiary. Death by hanging was used between 1899 and 1949, with the early hangings possibly taking place in the North Wagon Gate.

The Death House was removed in 1965, when prison inmates asked that it be taken down since the death penalty was abolished by the state of West Virginia. If you walk around once side of the Bull Pen area, you can make out a bit of the old foundation of the Death House.

The Exercise Area/Bullpen area where the Death House once stood
Photo by author 2009

Paranormal Activity: Feelings of sadness and dread. Several have felt what is described as static electricity on their arms and fingertips.

Proceed to the Wagon Gate area. You can see it from the Bull Pen area. It is an older style building with "Wagon Gate" painted on it.

Long Gone Buildings

Gone are many buildings that once occupied the yards. Once located in the North Recreation Yard were buildings used to produce prison products of brooms, tobacco, and clothes. There were two separate hospital buildings and a dining hall with chapel and a library: The Female Department, separate dining hall, and a shirt shop. A water tower also once stood near Guard Tower 4. There were also separate buildings for mail and laundry.

One of the many buildings which have been demolished
From the MEDC collection

Wagon Gate area

Located in the North Wall yard area is the Wagon Gate. This is a narrow two-story building which may have temporarily housed both men and women prisoners at one time. It is the oldest part of the prison. The wooden trap doors on the second floor may also have been the scene of several early hangings. (Don't explore upstairs as it is very dangerous due to the floor being very unstable)

The Wagon Gate is the original starting point for the building of the West Virginia Penitentiary, which was completed in Sept. 1866. The Wagon Gate housed nearly 100 convicts, who were used in the construction of the rest of the prison.

Paranormal activity: Shadows sighted, EVP'S captured

Wagon Gate in the North Yard
Photo by the Author 2011

If you leave the Wagon Gate area and walk outside toward the tallest center section of the prison, (it is four stories tall and is the administration area) you will soon be standing in front of the entrance to the Boiler Room. There are several steps down into this basement room. Be careful as they are uneven and tends to through you off balance.

Boiler Room *aka* the Hole

*The entrance to the Boiler Room
Photo by the Author 2013*

This is the series of rooms under the Administration building where Inmate Robert Daniel Wall met his death in 1979. It seems that there is a story about this man being a snitch as he was said to tell the guards whenever he caught the inmates engaging in illegal activity or breaking the rules. Some people say this is true and some say it is a falsity. Whatever the true tale we know one thing for sure. He died a violent death. He was killed by several prisoners one day while he was in the bathroom area of the Boiler Room. He was stabbed repeatedly with dull homemade prison knives until his blood was in puddles. His apparition has been claimed to be seen in the boiler room and around the entrance.

*The Boiler Room is located under this section of the Pen. Taken on an overnight investigation.
Photo by Author 2012*

Paranormal activity: This area tends to be a great spot for the capture of EVP. Many have heard whispers when no one is speaking. I saw a large shadow person at the entrance to this location and it was so life like it actually blocked out the sunshine from outside. This was not on a night event but at one of my Ghost hunting classes held in the early evening while the sun was still out.

If you investigate in colder months, be sure to hold your breath while taking photos. Your warm breath and a flash make for a spooky photo…but it won't be paranormal!

At the other far end of the Pen, there lies the South Wall (New Wall) and the South Yard. In the South Yard you will find the entrance to the Sugar Shack and you will see the Chapel building located outside.

South yard area

This is also where the entrance to the Sugar Shack is located. Head out door, past small booth area where the WV Pen radio station was located and to your left down ramp. Entrance to the Sugar Shack is down the steps.

As you exit the door from the hallway inside the Pen, go down the ramp and look to your right. You will see an outdoor restroom facility that the inmates used while outdoors. A man was attacked here and died. After that incident, the doors were taken off the stalls. No privacy when inmates needed to relieve themselves.

Paranormal activity: Several have reported capturing EVPs in this area.

Sugar Shack

The Sugar Shack entrance is in South Yard. As you walk through the large automatic doors near the lobby, turn to your right and look at the wall across from you. You will see a door that leads to the outside. This is the door to South Yard and the entrance to the Sugar Shack. Exit out the door. Walk down the ramp and then look for the steps that led down into another area. You are entering the Sugar Shack.

This was a room that was created for the purpose of recreation for the inmates when outside weather conditions would not permit them to go outdoors. It had a couple of pool tables and was not always supervised except for occasional checks by the guards. There are large cinder block columns in this room that could block ones line of vision. Two people could fit behind these columns and hide from the guards if need be. Why was it called the Sugar Shack? Well, they weren't handing out candy bars, I can assure you of that. It's been said that homosexual acts took place in the basement and that's where the name came from. I know...too much information.

*Taken back when the Pen was in operation
Photo from MEDC collection*

Though there were no deaths officially reported from the Sugar Shack, one can only imagine the violence that took place in there. Gambling, fighting and rape were normal occurrences to the prisoners within the walls of this room. As you walk around the Sugar Shack, you notice cartoons and some other paintings on the walls. Prisoners painted most of the artwork and it can be quite eerie in complete darkness. Most of the artwork is original, except for the Mothman like figures painted on the walls in dark paint. You can thank MTV's Fear show for that. They will not be permitted back on site due to defacing state property.

Sugar Shack on lower level of the Pen
Photo by Author 2006

Paranormal Activity:
Today, many investigations lead to paranormal discoveries in this particular area. Many unexplained noises and cold spots can also be felt in this particular area as well as numerous shadow people reports.

The Chapel Building

This was the non-denominational chapel where prisoners worshipped. This was built after the old Chapel was torn down.

Paranormal activity: a shadowy form has been seen darting behind the building and out of sight. Upon examination, no one is ever found behind the building.

Second Story

Medical Infirmary:

If you are outside, head back in. Find a staircase to get upstairs. You can access the steps by the Cafeteria hallway and Contact Visitation area. The other set of steps is down in the center part of the prison. Look for the "nice" floor tile and the Wheel device. Turn here and you will see the staircase that leads upstairs. Head up the stairs (across from the Wheel area) and you will soon be in the Medical Infirmary. The original Pen hospital and tuberculosis building were located in separate buildings out in the yard. The Medical Infirmary has some hot spots, of course. The main area seems to be the room with the dental equipment. Take time to snap some photos in here. We've gotten quite a few unusual anomalies in here but be careful of camera flash reflections in the windows. You will notice a room with a bathtub in it. There was a great EVP caught here in 2005. It said "I'm so cold." Interesting to note that one simple treatment for aggressive patients was to put them in bathtubs filled with ice cold water. Ever heard the term "chill out"? Now you know the rest of the story.

Walk into the large room and imagine wall to wall beds in here. This was a ward for the ill and would be filled to over capacity at times. The noises, the smells, and the pain of the past sometimes makes itself present here. Imagine being in prison and being sick. Communicable diseases ran rampant before antibiotics were invented. The prison saw its share of death with small pox, the Influenza epidemic of 1917-1918 and TB. Take some time to capture EVPS but beware of echoes in this room. At times, you can hear street noises from the outside as well.

My daughter, Sage Recco, captured her very first EVP in this area. It was during one of my Ghost hunting class's onsite. I had all females in class that night, not a single male was present. She turned on her recorder and began asking multiple questions. On the drive home that night, we played the tape back. I heard Sage ask, "Are you okay that we are here tonight?" and a man's whispered reply, "I loooove you." Talk about a great capture… but the look on Sage's face was priceless. It made a believer out of a skeptic!

Paranormal activity:
Shadow people, EVPs and anomalies in photographs.
(Specifically in the dental room) Various teams and investigators love the anomalies captured in various rooms in this area. One hotspot has been the room with the dental equipment, x-ray area, and there is also one door that slams itself on occasion. On one ghost hunt, it was secured, closed, and seemed jammed. When the investigators walked back thru minutes later, it was wide open and unlocked.

Continue walking thru the doors along the Medical Ward hallway.

Medical infirmary area with dental equipment
Photo by Author 2008

Psychiatric Ward

The Psychiatric area is located past the Medical Ward and is also on the second floor. It is one of my favorite places to investigate in the entire building although it can be blistering hot in the summer. We've recorded temps of 100 plus degrees on some hot summer nights.

The history of Psychiatry is a rather lengthy discussion and too involved to even touch on in this manual. I read a very large book on it while I was in nursing school and was shocked at the various treatments that were applied to patients throughout the earlier years. There was a great deal of experimentation in the field and some techniques were effective and many were not.

As any researcher worth their ectoplasm knows, where there is trauma, death and despair, the energy can at times be palpable to those who are sensitive. This can be an area of heaviness as well as paranormal activity. If you are sensitive, be aware.

Photo by Nicole Myers 2008. Mist and streaks on Psych Ward floor
From the MEDC collection

Paranormal Activity: EVP captures abound in this area. We have had multiple reports of whispers and of laughter when no one is present or speaking. Many reported sightings of shadows moving to and fro. Loud doors have slammed when no one is nearby. This was reported by a group called The Awakening Psychics; "While we were investigating the WV State Penitentiary, we were in the psych ward. A door opened by itself and we caught it on film. We did not see the door open however until we were home reviewing the footage. A year later we returned to the prison and did everything to duplicate the door opening without assistance. The door was a solid, heavy steel door and it does not open by without help."

This next two areas I feel I need to make mention of is due to the interest of many who ask about them. The first is the

Wardens Quarter. The second is the Gym. Both are on upper floors. Note these locations are not currently accessible to tour guests or overnight investigators. Sorry!

Wardens Quarters:

The second floor of the main entrance section housed the offices of the warden and others. The third and fourth floors were the warden's home with an open wood stairway. The Warden and family moved off this site in 1951.

The Wardens Quarters are not accessible to the public at the writing of this book. Damage to the ceiling, and crumbling plaster account for much of the damage over the past years. I have seen the area and can imagine how grand it must have been many years ago.

The Warden's Quarters
Photo by Author 2005

Gymnasium/Auditorium:

On the second floor over the honor hall is a gymnasium, which has hardwood floors marked for basketball. Inmate Mark Allen Parker was convicted of beating William Yakubik to death with a weight bar during a recreation period. This area used to be accessible but the floor is unstable and has heaved upward due to the possible leaking of water from the flat roof. There *may or may* not be access to this area during your investigation. Be cautious and aware if you do enter.

Paranormal activity: EVPs captured here. Watch out for dust orbs in your photographs. This is a very dusty floor. If you don't think so, shine your flashlight beam out in front of your face and watch the dust fly! Be sure to not walk out into the center of the gym floor too far.

Wardens Quarter. The second is the Gym. Both are on upper floors. Note these locations are not currently accessible to tour guests or overnight investigators. Sorry!

Wardens Quarters:

The second floor of the main entrance section housed the offices of the warden and others. The third and fourth floors were the warden's home with an open wood stairway. The Warden and family moved off this site in 1951.

The Wardens Quarters are not accessible to the public at the writing of this book. Damage to the ceiling, and crumbling plaster account for much of the damage over the past years. I have seen the area and can imagine how grand it must have been many years ago.

The Warden's Quarters
Photo by Author 2005

Gymnasium/Auditorium:

On the second floor over the honor hall is a gymnasium, which has hardwood floors marked for basketball. Inmate Mark Allen Parker was convicted of beating William Yakubik to death with a weight bar during a recreation period. This area used to be accessible but the floor is unstable and has heaved upward due to the possible leaking of water from the flat roof. There *may or may* not be access to this area during your investigation. Be cautious and aware if you do enter.

Paranormal activity: EVPs captured here. Watch out for dust orbs in your photographs. This is a very dusty floor. If you don't think so, shine your flashlight beam out in front of your face and watch the dust fly! Be sure to not walk out into the center of the gym floor too far.

CHAPTER 10
Electronic Voice Phenomena

Thomas Edison was intrigued by this unusual phenomena and was said to have been working on a Spirit Communicator when he passed from this world in October of 1931. He had announced in 1920 that he that he was working on a machine to open the lines of communication with the spirit world. In the aftermath of World War I, spiritualism was undergoing a revival, and many people hoped science could provide a means to access the souls of the recently deceased. Edison, himself an agnostic who admitted he had no idea if a spirit world even existed, spoke of his quest to communicate with spirit in several magazines. He explained to The New York Times that his machine would measure what he described as the life units that scatter through the universe after death. The communicator or any written plans were never found.

Frederick Jurgenson is credited with the name of EVP and was the first person to recognize and document this so called supernatural occurrence. Many have followed in their footsteps and successfully captured the spirit voices that are unattainable by the human ear unless recorded on tape.

How did all of this come about? Jurgenson was audiotaping bird songs in Sweden in the summer of 1959 when on playback he heard the voice of his dead mother calling him by his "pet" name that only she used.

Electronic Voice Phenomena is one of those occurrences that I truly believe you need to try few times for yourself before making a decision on whether this is the possible, or impossible. Any location inside the prison will work for your EVP session. Just be sure it is quiet and away from others who may be exploring. You don't want their voices or whispers to taint your evidence.

Grab your something to record audio. It can be an old school cassette recorder (use fresh tapes) a digital voice recorder or even a cell phone with a sound recorder will work in a pinch. People have actually captured EVP while using a video camera.

Here is a suggestion of EVP questions that you could ask. Speak into your recorder plainly and state what time it is and what area you are inside of. This helps on [play back to help you know what are you were in when and if you capture a voice.

Is there anyone here?
Can you give me your name?
What age are you?
Where you an inmate?
If you were an inmate, what was your crime?
Were you really guilty of it?
Do you have a message for me?
What is your inmate number?
How did you die?
Do you have any regrets?
Do you like having me here?
How was the food here?
How may were in your cell?

Did you ever try to escape?
Did you experience pain here?
What happened to you?
Were you a model prisoner?

If you are a female and want to ask these questions below, be prepared for whatever the response may be.

For females to ask in an EVP session:
I'm a woman. Did you miss women while you were a prisoner?
Were you lonely?
Do you like me?

    EVP sessions should really only last a few minutes in each location. I believe that 5-10 minutes is enough time to get a capture. I believe that YOUR energy and THEIR energy is at the greatest for about the first five minutes after you enter the area.

    Speak in a normal tone. Do not whisper. If you whisper, be sure to note this on the recorder as "I am whispering" or you may get confused later and hear something a human said and thinks it is a spirit voice. Also, if another group comes thru your area, be sure to note it like this " I'm hearing footsteps and voices from another group."

    On playback, it's best to use headphones and crank up the sound. You will need to listen several times. EVP can be vague and hard to hear. Listen and also have another set of ears listen as well so you do not miss anything.

    My favorite EVP at the prison? My beautiful and innocent teenage daughter capturing a male voice whispering, "I love you". Simply eerie! Good luck with your EVP sessions. Let the recordings begin.

CHAPTER 11
PARANORMAL INVESTIGATION FORMS

So you have planned to investigate the West Virginia Pen? Documenting your experiences is a goal that nearly all paranormal investigators attain. The next few pages are to help guide you and hopefully help you to organize your investigation. Whether you are on a private investigation or a public ghost hunt, these pages will be helpful.

Grab a pen and start documenting!

West Virginia Pen Investigation

Members/Individuals present:

Date of investigation:

Start time of investigation:

End time of investigation:

Equipment used:

Lunar Phase on this date:

Temperature outdoors:

Temperature indoors:

Wind speed: (if it's windy enough to rattle loose window panes, note this.

Humidity level:

Solar Flares?
(consult the NOAA website on your smartphone)

Geo Magnetic Storms?

Meteor showers?

Venture into each area and spend some time with your equipment. Note anything out of the ordinary that you feel or other team members experience in the NOTE section.

Lobby/Museum area:

EMF Readings?

Base temperature?

Any temperature spikes or low readings?

EVP's?

Any anomalies in digital photographs?

Any video anomalies?

Any voices other than team members heard? If so, explain.

Any sounds you could not explain? Radio playing? Music box heard?

Cell door slamming?

Any moving shadows that you could not explain?

Did anyone visually see orbs?

Any unusual lights?

Strong random thoughts or names that "came suddenly" to you?

Unusual smells? Explain.

Sensation of being watched?

Dowsing results?

Any electrical disturbances? Lights going on off? Equipment malfunctioning? Battery issues?

Are there any renovations going on in this area?

Anything physical happen that you could not explain? Hair pulled? Shoulder touched? Leg grabbed? (it happens!)

Psychic Impressions?

<u>Non Contact Visitation room</u> (by lobby)

EMF Readings?

Base temperature?

Any temperature spikes or low readings?

EVP's?

Any anomalies in digital photographs?

Any video anomalies?

Any voices other than team members heard? If so, explain.

Any sounds you could not explain? Radio playing? Music box heard?

Cell door slamming?

Any moving shadows that you could not explain?

Did anyone visually see orbs?

Any unusual lights?

Strong random thoughts or names that "came suddenly" to you?

Unusual smells? Explain.

Sensation of being watched?

Dowsing results?

Any electrical disturbances? Lights going on off? Equipment malfunctioning? Battery issues?

Are there any renovations going on in this area?

Anything physical happen that you could not explain? Hair pulled? Shoulder touched? Leg grabbed? (it happens!)

Psychic Impressions

Hall outside of the Lobby:

EMF Readings?

Base temperature?

Any temperature spikes or low readings?

EVP's?

Any anomalies in digital photographs?

Any video anomalies?

Any voices other than team members heard? If so, explain.

Any sounds you could not explain? Radio playing? Music box heard?

Cell door slamming?

Any moving shadows that you could not explain?

Did anyone visually see orbs?

Any unusual lights?

Strong random thoughts or names that "came suddenly" to you?

Unusual smells? Explain.

Sensation of being watched?

Dowsing results?

Any electrical disturbances? Lights going on off? Equipment malfunctioning? Battery issues?

Are there any renovations going on in this area?

Anything physical happen that you could not explain? Hair pulled? Shoulder touched? Leg grabbed? (it happens!)

Psychic Impressions

Contact Visitation room:

EMF Readings?

Base temperature?

Any temperature spikes or low readings?

EVP's?

Any anomalies in digital photographs?

Any video anomalies?

Any voices other than team members heard? If so, explain.

Any sounds you could not explain? Radio playing? Music box heard?

Cell door slamming?

Any moving shadows that you could not explain?

Did anyone visually see orbs?

Any unusual lights?

Strong random thoughts or names that "came suddenly" to you?

Unusual smells? Explain.

Sensation of being watched?

Dowsing results?

Any electrical disturbances? Lights going on off? Equipment malfunctioning? Battery issues?

Are there any renovations going on in this area?

Anything physical happen that you could not explain? Hair pulled? Shoulder touched? Leg grabbed? (it happens!)

Psychic Impressions

Cafeteria Hallway:

EMF Readings?

Base temperature?

Any temperature spikes or low readings?

EVP's?

Any anomalies in digital photographs?

Any video anomalies?

Any voices other than team members heard? If so, explain.

Any sounds you could not explain? Radio playing? Music box heard?

Cell door slamming?

Any moving shadows that you could not explain?

Did anyone visually see orbs?

Any unusual lights?

Strong random thoughts or names that "came suddenly" to you?

Unusual smells? Explain.

Sensation of being watched?

Dowsing results?
Any electrical disturbances? Lights going on off? Equipment malfunctioning? Battery issues?

Are there any renovations going on in this area?

Anything physical happen that you could not explain? Hair pulled? Shoulder touched? Leg grabbed? (it happens!)

Psychic Impressions

Cafeteria:

EMF Readings?

Base temperature?

Any temperature spikes or low readings?

EVP's?

Any anomalies in digital photographs?

Any video anomalies?

Any voices other than team members heard? If so, explain.

Any sounds you could not explain? Radio playing? Music box heard?

Cell door slamming?

Any moving shadows that you could not explain?

Did anyone visually see orbs?

Any unusual lights?

Strong random thoughts or names that "came suddenly" to you?

Unusual smells? Explain.
Sensation of being watched?

Dowsing results?

Any electrical disturbances? Lights going on off? Equipment malfunctioning? Battery issues?

Are there any renovations going on in this area?

Anything physical happen that you could not explain? Hair pulled? Shoulder touched? Leg grabbed? (it happens!)

Psychic Impressions

Kitchen area:

EMF Readings?

Base temperature?

Any temperature spikes or low readings?

EVP's?

Any anomalies in digital photographs?

Any video anomalies?

Any voices other than team members heard? If so, explain.

Any sounds you could not explain? Radio playing? Music box heard?

Cell door slamming?

Any moving shadows that you could not explain?

Did anyone visually see orbs?

Any unusual lights?

Strong random thoughts or names that "came suddenly" to you?

Unusual smells? Explain.

Sensation of being watched?

Dowsing results?

Any electrical disturbances? Lights going on off? Equipment malfunctioning? Battery issues?

Are there any renovations going on in this area?

Anything physical happen that you could not explain? Hair pulled? Shoulder touched? Leg grabbed? (it happens!)

Psychic Impressions

The Wheel area:

EMF Readings?

Base temperature?

Any temperature spikes or low readings?

EVP's?

Any anomalies in digital photographs?
Any video anomalies?

Any voices other than team members heard? If so, explain.

Any sounds you could not explain? Radio playing? Music box heard?

Cell door slamming?

Any moving shadows that you could not explain?

Did anyone visually see orbs?

Any unusual lights?

Strong random thoughts or names that "came suddenly" to you?

Unusual smells? Explain.

Sensation of being watched?

Dowsing results?

Any electrical disturbances? Lights going on off? Equipment malfunctioning? Battery issues?

Are there any renovations going on in this area?

Anything physical happen that you could not explain? Hair pulled? Shoulder touched? Leg grabbed? (it happens!)

Psychic Impressions

North Hall:

EMF Readings?

Base temperature?

Any temperature spikes or low readings?

EVP's?

Any anomalies in digital photographs?

Any video anomalies?

Any voices other than team members heard? If so, explain.

Any sounds you could not explain? Radio playing? Music box heard?

Cell door slamming?

Any moving shadows that you could not explain?

Did anyone visually see orbs?

Any unusual lights?

Strong random thoughts or names that "came suddenly" to you?

Unusual smells? Explain.

Sensation of being watched?

Dowsing results?

Any electrical disturbances? Lights going on off? Equipment malfunctioning? Battery issues?

Are there any renovations going on in this area?

Anything physical happen that you could not explain? Hair pulled? Shoulder touched? Leg grabbed? (it happens!)

Psychic Impressions

Medical Infirmary 2nd floor:

EMF Readings?

Base temperature?

Any temperature spikes or low readings?

EVP's?

Any anomalies in digital photographs?

Any video anomalies?

Any voices other than team members heard? If so, explain.

Any sounds you could not explain? Radio playing? Music box heard?

Cell door slamming?

Any moving shadows that you could not explain?

Did anyone visually see orbs?
Any unusual lights?

Strong random thoughts or names that "came suddenly" to you?

Unusual smells? Explain.

Sensation of being watched?

Dowsing results?

Any electrical disturbances? Lights going on off? Equipment malfunctioning? Battery issues?

Are there any renovations going on in this area?

Anything physical happen that you could not explain? Hair pulled? Shoulder touched? Leg grabbed? (it happens!)

Psychic Impressions

Psychiatric Ward 2nd floor:

EMF Readings?

Base temperature?

Any temperature spikes or low readings?

EVP's?

Any anomalies in digital photographs?

Any video anomalies?

Any voices other than team members heard? If so, explain.

Any sounds you could not explain? Radio playing? Music box heard?

Cell door slamming?

Any moving shadows that you could not explain?

Did anyone visually see orbs?

Any unusual lights?

Strong random thoughts or names that "came suddenly" to you?

Unusual smells? Explain.

Sensation of being watched?

Dowsing results?

Any electrical disturbances? Lights going on off? Equipment malfunctioning? Battery issues?

Are there any renovations going on in this area?

Anything physical happen that you could not explain? Hair pulled? Shoulder touched? Leg grabbed? (it happens!)

Psychic Impressions

South Hall (New Wall):

EMF Readings?

Base temperature?

Any temperature spikes or low readings?

EVP's?

Any anomalies in digital photographs?

Any video anomalies?

Any voices other than team members heard? If so, explain.

Any sounds you could not explain? Radio playing? Music box heard?

Cell door slamming?

Any moving shadows that you could not explain?

Did anyone visually see orbs?

Any unusual lights?

Strong random thoughts or names that "came suddenly" to you?

Unusual smells? Explain.

Sensation of being watched?

Dowsing results?

Any electrical disturbances? Lights going on off? Equipment malfunctioning? Battery issues?

Are there any renovations going on in this area?

Anything physical happen that you could not explain? Hair pulled? Shoulder touched? Leg grabbed? (it happens!)

Psychic Impressions

Sugar Shack lower level:

EMF Readings?

Base temperature?

Any temperature spikes or low readings?

EVP's?

Any anomalies in digital photographs?

Any video anomalies?

Any voices other than team members heard? If so, explain.

Any sounds you could not explain? Radio playing? Music box heard?

Cell door slamming?

Any moving shadows that you could not explain?

Did anyone visually see orbs?

Any unusual lights?

Strong random thoughts or names that "came suddenly" to you?

Unusual smells? Explain.

Sensation of being watched?

Dowsing results?

Any electrical disturbances? Lights going on off? Equipment malfunctioning? Battery issues?

Are there any renovations going on in this area?

Anything physical happen that you could not explain? Hair pulled? Shoulder touched? Leg grabbed? (it happens!)

Psychic Impressions

Boiler Room aka The Hole on lower level;

EMF Readings?

Base temperature?

Any temperature spikes or low readings?

EVP's?

Any anomalies in digital photographs?

Any video anomalies?

Any voices other than team members heard? If so, explain.

Any sounds you could not explain? Radio playing? Music box heard?

Cell door slamming?

Any moving shadows that you could not explain?

Did anyone visually see orbs?

Any unusual lights?

Strong random thoughts or names that "came suddenly" to you?

Unusual smells? Explain.

Sensation of being watched?

Dowsing results?

Any electrical disturbances? Lights going on off? Equipment malfunctioning? Battery issues?

Are there any renovations going on in this area?

Anything physical happen that you could not explain?

Hair pulled? Shoulder touched? Leg grabbed? (it happens!)

Psychic Impressions

Wagon Gate area –North Yard-Outdoors;

EMF Readings?

Base temperature?
Any temperature spikes or low readings?

EVP's?

Any anomalies in digital photographs?

Any video anomalies?

Any voices other than team members heard? If so, explain.

Any sounds you could not explain? Radio playing? Music box heard?

Cell door slamming?

Any moving shadows that you could not explain?
Did anyone visually see orbs?

Any unusual lights?

Strong random thoughts or names that "came suddenly" to you?

Unusual smells? Explain.

Sensation of being watched?

Dowsing results?

Any electrical disturbances? Lights going on off? Equipment malfunctioning? Battery issues?

Are there any renovations going on in this area?

Anything physical happen that you could not explain? Hair pulled? Shoulder touched? Leg grabbed? (it happens!)

Psychic Impressions

Bullpen area-North Yard-(Death House once stood here)- Outdoors;

EMF Readings?

Base temperature?

Any temperature spikes or low readings?

EVP's?

Any anomalies in digital photographs?

Any video anomalies?

Any voices other than team members heard? If so, explain.

Any sounds you could not explain? Radio playing? Music box heard?

Cell door slamming?

Any moving shadows that you could not explain?

Did anyone visually see orbs?
Any unusual lights?
Strong random thoughts or names that "came suddenly" to you?

Unusual smells? Explain.

Sensation of being watched?

Dowsing results?

Any electrical disturbances? Lights going on off? Equipment malfunctioning? Battery issues?

Are there any renovations going on in this area?

Anything physical happen that you could not explain? Hair pulled? Shoulder touched? Leg grabbed? (it happens!)

Psychic Impressions

Exercise area and Chapel building area-South Yard— Outdoors;

EMF Readings?

Base temperature?

Any temperature spikes or low readings?

EVP's?

Any anomalies in digital photographs?

Any video anomalies?

Any voices other than team members heard? If so, explain.

Any sounds you could not explain? Radio playing? Music box heard?

Cell door slamming?
Any moving shadows that you could not explain?

Did anyone visually see orbs?

Any unusual lights?

Strong random thoughts or names that "came suddenly" to you?

Unusual smells? Explain.

Sensation of being watched?

Dowsing results?

Any electrical disturbances? Lights going on off? Equipment malfunctioning? Battery issues?

Are there any renovations going on in this area?

Anything physical happen that you could not explain? Hair pulled? Shoulder touched? Leg grabbed? (it happens!)

Psychic Impressions

Miscellaneous areas investigated not listed here:
EMF Readings?
Base temperature?
Any temperature spikes or low readings?
EVP's?
Any anomalies in digital photographs?
Any video anomalies?
Any voices other than team members heard? If so, explain.
Any sounds you could not explain? Radio playing? Music

box heard?

Cell door slamming?

Any moving shadows that you could not explain?

Did anyone visually see orbs?

Any unusual lights?

Strong random thoughts or names that "came suddenly" to you?

Unusual smells? Explain.

Sensation of being watched?

Dowsing results?

Any electrical disturbances? Lights going on off? Equipment malfunctioning? Battery issues?

Are there any renovations going on in this area?

Anything physical happen that you could not explain? Hair pulled? Shoulder touched? Leg grabbed? (it happens!)

Psychic Impression?

NOTES:

Results of your completed investigation:

Most active area investigated:

Conclusion of investigation:

Be as precise and factual as possible, trying not to use conjecture (stick to the evidence and don't make assumptions about the results). Don't forget to specify what you did & what equipment you may have used to form your hypothesis.

Congratulations on your investigation of the West Virginia Penitentiary. You made it!

CONCLUSION

There are numerous locations in the world that claim to have paranormal activity. We wish you well as you explore the paranormal field and continue to learn the history, albeit a bit dark, of each location you choose. We hope that you return to explore the infamous West Virginia Pen once more.

Happy hauntings and we hope to see you on the ghost hunting trail! Now go get busy investigating.

To visit the official West Virginia Penitentiary website visit:
www.wvpentours.com

To visit the Author's website, purchase books or join her on a ghost hunt visit: www.HauntedHistory.net

To read the Author's blog visit:
www.SherriBrake.blogspot.com

Ghost Hunters Guide to the West Virginia Pen

MAPS OF THE WEST VIRGINIA PENITENTIARY

Ground level

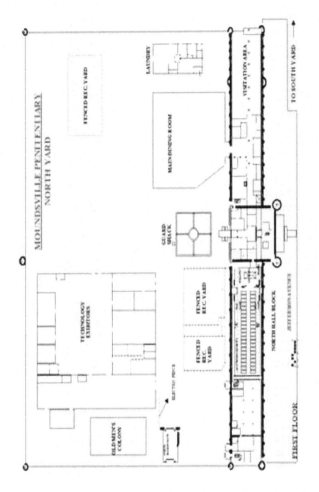

North Yard

Entrance to Boiler room, Wagon Gate building and Bullpen/outdoor exercise area where Death House stood. (this is shown as fenced recreation yard.) Outside entrance to North Hall.

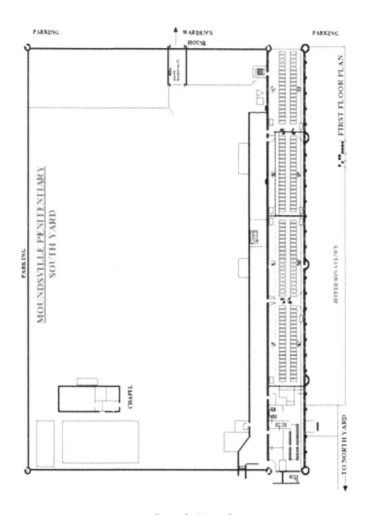

South Yard

Chapel, entrance to Sugar Shack, outdoor inmate restrooms (non-functioning)

ABOUT THE AUTHOR

Walking the shadow-filled hallways of historical and haunted buildings is the stuff dreams are made of if you are a paranormal researcher and a history lover. It's a dream come true for author, paranormal class instructor and columnist, Sherri Brake. She began researching the odd and unusual several decades ago and enjoys bringing people along on her overnight ghost hunt adventures.

Sherri lives in central West Virginia on a 100 acre farm with her husband, a bunch of chickens, several cats, a coonhound and one elusive ghost. She is the mother of two children who are not afraid of the dark, thanks to their mom.

Check out her website at www.HauntedHistory.net

Made in the USA
Columbia, SC
10 July 2018